ATLANTA
A City Of Neighborhoods

ATLANTA
A City Of Neighborhoods

Joseph F. Thompson
Photography

Robert Isbell
Narrative

University Of South Carolina Press

Copyright © 1994 University of South Carolina

Published in Columbia, South Carolina by the University of South Carolina Press
Manufactured in the United States of America

Library of Congress Cataloging-in-Publication Data

Thompson, Joseph F., 1931 -
     Atlanta: a city of neighborhoods / photography by Joseph F.
Thompson : narrative by Robert Isbell.
            p.   cm.
     Includes index.
     ISBN 0-87249-979-0 (hardback : acid-free)
     1. Atlanta (Ga.) – Pictorial works.   2. Atlanta (Ga.) – Social life
and customs.   3. Neighborhood – Georgia – Atlanta.   4. Neighborhood –
Georgia – Atlanta – Pictorial works.   I. Isbell, Robert, 1923 -
II. Title
F294.A843T48   1993
975.8' 231– dc20   93-8089

In recognition of the vision
and courage of all those
who have enabled Atlanta
to accomodate great social
and economic change while
preserving the charm
of its Southern past.

Acknowledgements

Special thanks to the following people without whose help this book would not have been possible:

Atlanta Historic Center – Franklin Garrett, Don Rooney, Helen Matthews, and Ann Falter. *Atlanta Preservation Center* – Carson Pease, Anne Farrisee. *Atlanta Urban Design Commission* – Karen Huebner and Susan Gwinner. *Georgia Trust For Historic Preservation* – Tommy Jones.

Those in the neighborhoods who are not mentioned in the narrative: *Adair Park* – Jeanne Mills and Richard Mueller. *Candler Park* – Randy Pimsler. *Druid Hills* – Dr. Richard Groepper. *Grant Park* – Cliff Alterkruse. *Inman Park* – Carol Mitchell. *Kirkwood* – Wayne Carey. *Mechanicsville* – Rosa Burney. *Midtown* –David Rhinehart. *Morningside/Lenox Park* – Syd Janney, Larrie Del Martin, Becky Vaughn. *Old Fourth Ward* – Charles Mize. *Peoplestown* – Ethel Mae Matthews. *Pittsburgh* – Imogene Shannon. *Virginia-Highland* – Betsy and Burn Sears. *Whittier Mills* – Laura Lieberman.

Those who helped in a variety of ways:

Fran Isbell for proofreading, Sandra Hermann for her hospitality and neighborhood guidance, Marina Neal for supplying research material, and Sarah Lapinel for her support and talent early in the project.

Images on pages 11, 12, 13, 14, 21, 47, 53, 55, 99, 118 courtesy of the *Atlanta History Center.*

Contents

ATLANTA
A City Of Neighborhoods

Man is a political creature
and one whose nature is to live with others.
                              Aristotle, *Ethics*

Preface

Peachtree Battle

If its pages were to include all Atlanta neighborhoods, this book would be an overstatement of more than a dozen times its current size. As presented, however, the words and pictures take a reader through twenty-six carefully chosen communities that together tell a story of the whole city.

■   ■   ■

From the beginning of its tumultuous history, Atlanta has bred valor, resilience, and consummate gentility. Although drugs, thievery, violence, and poverty run high (as in any metropolis), there is an indefinable poise that runs throughout – from the penury of Reynoldstown to the affluence of Tuxedo Park.

A civil evenness seems to mark the ways of neighborhood leaders, no matter the section they represent. It is as though some Johnny Appleseed person once strode through and cast about copies of a book that reminded Atlantans how to be fair under stress.

Its people have watched dreams soar, plummet, and then rise again.

Through this culture there simmers quite near the surface the love for one's own spot of earth. Regardless of their privation or wealth, neighbors of any Atlanta community sooner or later come together to defend their habitats. While they may love Atlanta to the point of chauvinism, these neighbors routinely fight City Hall. Often, in defense of their domiciles, they oppose measures that could make the city larger and more prosperous. The quest of these otherwise forbearing people to keep their neighborhoods pure – according to their own concepts – can be at times intense and overwhelming.

There can be little question: Atlanta has time and again risen above its ravages. For much more than a century and a half, its people have watched dreams soar, plummet, and then rise again. Leaders of more placid Southern cities snicker at the image of Atlanta's apparent swagger; yet they conceal awe for the symmetry with which Atlanta's leaders deal with their city's growth and social issues. Local citizens like to quote late Mayor William B. Hartsfield: "Atlanta is a city too busy to hate."

∎ ∎ ∎

William B. Hartsfield, mayor 1937-61, the drive behind Atlanta's aviation growth.

Only twenty-five years before the Civil War, an army engineer drove a pine stake into the soil of rural Georgia to mark the southeastern extreme of a planned rail line in the area that would one day be Atlanta's Five Points. Officials called the rustic locale Terminus. Within six years a small outpost grew up here, and a Georgia governor named the village Marthasville in honor of a daughter. The modest settlement then flowered and by 1845 became known as Atlanta; but within twenty years, in the late summer of 1864, Northern invaders drove people from their homes and torched the burgeoning city – ironically, in tandem with retreating Southern troops.

The Cotton States and International Exposition, 1895

Just thirty years later, without federal aid or assurance of outside help, Atlanta announced to the world that it would hold a mammoth event the following summer. The extravaganza would be to the South in 1895 what Chicago's Columbian Exposition had been to the Midwest in 1893.

Walter G. Cooper was to write in 1896 that the undertaking was "...one of the finest examples of American pluck." The Cotton States and International Exposition came into being on the heels of an economic panic; it was without appreciable capital support, and occurred at a time when killing debt loads strapped the city's bankers.

The exposition spread over Piedmont Park like the Toledo of El Greco's painting. Visitors came not only from the South but (happily welcomed by S. M. Inman and fellow exposition promoters) from New England, the Middle Atlantic, the East, and the Midwest. Besides luring outside wealth for industrial expansion, the event brought talented people from Mississippi, Alabama, Tennessee, and the Carolinas. These were young lions who found only scant challenges within the struggling communities and piney woods of Reconstruction times. After the exposition, many remained in a buoyant new Atlanta and became architects, engineers, writers, artists, doctors, lawyers, merchants, real estate developers. As the new century arrived, they meshed their ingenuity with that of the aging giants of the passing century, and with èlan they drove Atlanta to higher ground.

New prosperity adorned Atlanta with the rise of Victorian castles, country estates, social clubs, tall buildings, and sprawling industrial plants.

An obscure druggist formulated the Coca-Cola drink in 1886 and sold it two years later to future philanthropist Asa Candler. This enterprise, along with expanding rail activity and the roar of new industries, swelled the city with people.

Where once executives and laborers walked daily to work from neighborhoods abutting the commercial district, they now began to move out from the hub. At that time, a few commuted by train from new homes on the outskirts such as a small railroad stop called Kirkwood on the edge of General Gordon's estate.

Then people like George Washington Adair, a daring business gambler, caught the drift of the city's spread. Adair reasoned that Atlanta would soon cease to be a walking city; he would run horsecar lines to his new developments and make them attractive for those who found it harder day-by-day to buy homes in the inner borough. Although Adair twice lost his fortunes, he, like the city itself, came back. His real estate empire, later guided by two sons, expanded to be the largest in the city by World War I.

Horsecars were only a stopgap for the times. The poor animals, pulling 30 or 40 passengers along rails, strained to exhaustion on hills; often they stumbled and fell. There was a better way in the offing, and promoters like Adair and the enterprising Joel Hurt found the answer in the newly invented electric trolley. This, plus the arrival of the horseless carriage, hastened suburbia's growth.

Philip Shutze, a Rome Prize scholar, who with his mentor, Neel Reid, most influenced the architectural styles of the city's grand homes.

Adair reasoned that Atlanta would soon cease to be a walking city.

Although whites and blacks sometimes lived in the same areas, Jim Crow laws separated the citizens, and it was not until after World War II that minorities slowly began to move into white neighborhoods.

For various reasons, whites began leaving their homes, moving to the outskirts, often into towns beyond the city's boundaries. Many felt, justifiably, that property values would decline and schools would be dominated by the sheer numbers of a race long denied equal citizenship. Such circumstances were not just the province of Atlanta and the South but, to one degree or another, existed throughout America. For minorities and blue-collar Caucasians, "white flight" became a bonanza. They moved into the vacated Victorian homes and Craftsman Bungalows. Yet most affluent whites stayed because the value of properties far exceeded the buying means of low-income groups. Even where inroads were made into the more exclusive areas, young, mostly white executives and professional people soon found bargains. They bought into the now impoverished communities and renovated homes next door to poor and struggling neighbors. When landlords later raised rents, their vacating tenants charged "displacement."

Nevertheless, in the most modest neighborhoods, the minority population soared. Atlanta's public schools, abandoned by whites, grew to a black majority of nine to one by the 1990s.

Because of an abiding dialogue between blacks and whites – mostly inspired by peacemakers like the Rev. Martin Luther King, Jr., Coca-Cola magnate Robert Woodruff, and former Mayor Ivan Allen, Jr. – Atlanta escaped the early civil violence of a Los Angeles or a Detroit. Black residents still crowd the inner city and white homeowners still migrate outward, but in the main a neighborhood is shaped by personal economics. An outsider might be astonished to hear leaders of an affluent neighborhood boast that they live in an eclectic community of "Jews, gentiles, gays, blacks, singles, mixed-marrieds..." On the other hand, black leaders might tell you that although their neighborhoods suffer from neglect and poverty they expect a better world when whites return.

George W. Adair headed the city's first real estate empire.

Below:
The trolley to Inman Park, one of the early enterprises of real estate visionary Joel Hurt.

Right:
Joel Hurt

Clearly, the collective attitude of Atlantans is to get on with improving human life and put past differences to rest. Today's issues center upon knotty love-hate face-offs. There are those who at times fight for the prosperity and growth of a total Atlanta; yet at other times they might rise up to challenge any growth that threatens their own backyards. Atlanta's quest to become a shining international city may well rest upon these resolves.

When in 1974 Maynard Jackson became the city's first black mayor, he quickly moved to soften neighborhood restlessness. He wanted citizens to know the problems and the political realities of a bulging metropolis; in turn, he assured them that City Council would come to know the issues that plagued the neighborhoods. He formed Neighborhood Planning Units and asked citizens not to come complaining if they did not have a plan.

Some homeowners bonded quickly and made their wishes known. Because they paid more taxes, affluent combatants were able to stop

Left:
Robert Woodruff, the man who drove Coca-Cola to prominence; Atlanta's most influential citizen.

Middle:
Ivan Allen, Jr. For eight years he guided the city through its greatest trials and most spectacular gains. Here with his wife, Louise Richardson Allen.

Right:
Martin Luther King, Jr.

the laying down of superhighways through their plush environs; there were poor communities, too, like Summerhill, Reynoldstown, and Kirkwood who could not afford costly legal help – yet they were aweless, and were known to fight City Hall and win.

Cleta Winslow, the spirited coordinator of Atlanta's NPUs, recognizes that areas like Summerhill have gone through a generation of decline, "But they are now mad, and I'm happy; it means they've become organized; when that happens, they can get things done." She says that time out for talk is finished and that all neighborhoods now must get down to business:

"When I talk to folks in the neighborhood, I say, 'Look, this is your life's work – not a one-month deal. Whether you know it or not, this is for life.' "

An oddity pervades all neighborhoods: Residents love Atlanta as a total city; they boost its growth and prosperity; they decry its misfortunes, but they often rear up against taxes, bond issues and other measures that might improve the city even to the slightest detriment of their own turf. How well the city can contain quality at both philosophical ends may determine Atlanta's place in the twenty-first century

■ ■ ■

On nights of a weekend, the city's young come to the bars, gardens, and sidewalks of the suburbs. Often in exotic dress they stroll about Little Five Points; in more conventional clothes they crowd the commercial blocks of Buckhead. They bring color and life to the edge of the neighborhoods, and for the time the venue is mostly theirs–places that are at the same time homesteads for some, free zones for others.

While many neighborhoods are private and seldom visited by the curious, there are in Atlanta a few places like Buckhead that are claimed by the world. When northsiders go outside the city, they are likely to tell an inquirer they are from Buckhead; inside the city they might say they are from Haynes Manor or Peachtree Heights. They do not exaggerate, for Buckhead is not a single neighborhood; it is a loose cluster of prestige residential areas, and it has its own shopping district. Like the Cyclorama, Stone Mountain, Six Flags, and historic Oakland Cemetery, Buckhead is the possession of all who claim it. Because the boundaries of its domain are drawn only in the eye of the beholder, Buckhead is not defined as a neighborhood in this book.

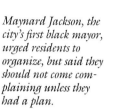

Maynard Jackson, the city's first black mayor, urged residents to organize, but said they should not come complaining unless they had a plan.

Cleta Winslow, coordinator of Neighborhood Planning Units

Little Five Points, a shopping area claimed by five neighborhoods

*Leisure time in
Buckhead's business
district*

**Buckhead: Not
a neighborhood
but the brightest
galaxy in the
Atlanta sky.**

*Right:
The Peachtree Cafe*

*The unusual Jasper
Smith monument in
Oakland Cemetery*

2500
Rivers Road

2824
Habersham Road

17

Above:
70 Muscogee

Right:
2700 Habersham
Road

18

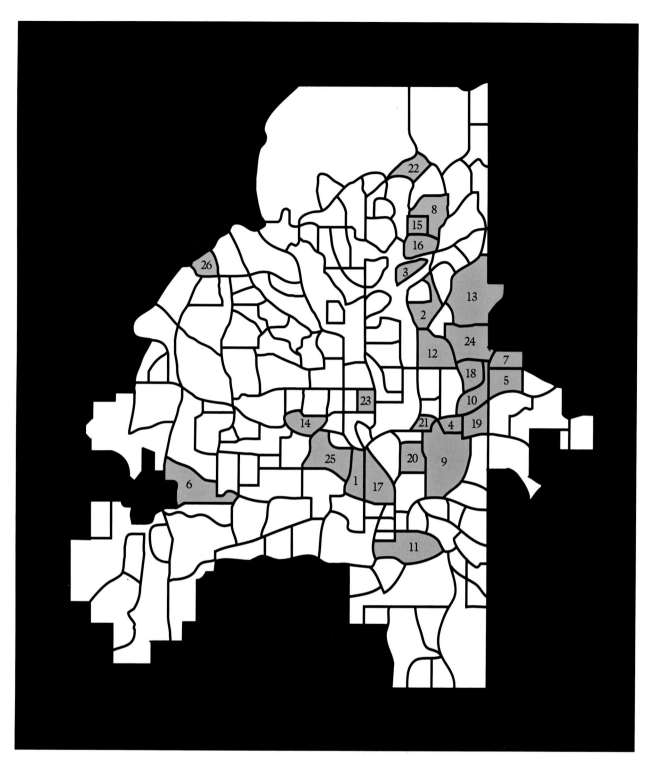

1. Adair Park	10. Inman Park	18. Poncey-Highland
2. Ansley Park	11. Lakewood Heights	19. Reynoldstown
3. Brookwood Hills	12. Midtown	20. Summerhill
4. Cabbagetown	13. Morningside-Lenox Park	21. Sweet Auburn
5. Candler Park		22. Tuxedo Park
6. Cascade Heights	14. Mozley Park	23. Vine City
7. Druid Hills	15. Peachtree Heights	24. Virginia-Highland
8. Garden Hills	16. Peachtree Hills	25. West End
9. Grant Park	17. Pittsburgh	26. Whittier Mills

Adair Park

In the quiet of early morning, when mist obscures the age-spots of tree-shaded homes, the streets become the spectre of the century's young years. Few places in America are so similar in style as the dwellings in the whole of Adair Park. They speak of an era when their residents were the heart of Atlanta's middle-class. They recall, too, the grand days of the city's most powerful real estate dynasty.

Adair Park was named for George Washington Adair, who at the age of twenty-two became a conductor on the Georgia Railroad. Modestly, at first, Adair began to build capital; by 1861 he had enough funds to help found *The Southern Confederacy*, a local newspaper of the Civil War era.

For the last two years of the Civil War, Adair was a colonel and aide-de-camp to his friend, General Nathan Bedford Forrest. When the war ended, Adair opened a wholesale grocery business and then a real estate office. From a terminal in the West End development – which Adair named for a district in London – he established a line of mule-drawn streetcars to run to the district that is today called Midtown.

Adair Park #1

Brian Robinson and Brendon Rowe

Lexington Avenue

It was from the latter experience that Adair formulated the idea of developing residences along streetcar lines. His fortune grew upon the concept, but Adair became bankrupt in the panic of 1873. Quickly he returned to buying and selling properties and running streetcar lines. By 1877 he had overextended his street railway and was bankrupt again.

Upon Adair's death in 1899, sons Forrest (named for the general) and George guided the Adair real estate enterprise into the new century. In the twenties, when the firm reached its zenith, all of Atlanta felt the impact of the Adair empire. The company achieved annual billings of $15 million.

Those who grew up in segregated Adair Park now live in harmony with people of several races who came here to buy affordable homes. Together they make up a vigorous neighborhood group called Adair Park Today. As in many residential areas, the influence of landscape architect Frederick Law Olmsted prevails, but the whole environment is a lingering reminder of George Washington Adair and sons Forrest and George.

The Abner G. Gillette Mansion, built in 1892-1894. Now owned by Robert Taylor.

George Washington Adair

Ansley Park

Business district as seen from Ansley Park's 15th Street

Hundreds of men, working with primitive tools and with mules and wagons, created a free-flowing garden of two hundred and seventy-five acres.

From Jane Price Harmon's home, one looks through the valley of great trees below and recalls New York's Central Park South. Tall, shimmering buildings of downtown Atlanta rise just beyond. Of an evening, Jane's guests pause at her door to look back upon the splendor. Here the resemblance ends. Ansley Park is not just a garden and playground; it is a place beauty-seeking neighbors have called home for ninety-odd years.

Park living was the dream of Edwin P. Ansley, a bold venturer in ideas who backed aesthetic tastes with rare wealth. Inspired by Frederick Law Olmsted (who designed New York's Central Park and earlier sculpted the avenues and linear parks of Druid Hills), Ansley employed a gifted engineer to draw up a plan of development.

Solon Zachary Ruff worked from a tableau of forests and hills and streams. He decreed that the avenues follow the lay of the land. Within these contours he inked in more than six hundred lots of disparate sizes and shapes. He laid out the streets so they melded with the land upon which homes, parks, and playgrounds would be built.

46 Maddox

Edwin Ansley spent more than a half-million dollars – an enormous sum for the time – to trim forests, drain swamps, cut driveways, and pave streets. Hundreds of men, working with primitive tools and with mules and wagons, created a free-flowing garden of two hundred and seventy-five acres. Long before they were finished, handsome homes were being erected – bungalows, two-story houses, and even mansions.

For himself, Ansley chose a three-acre homesite at the highest point. He hired noted architect Ten Eyck Brown to design a ten thousand square-foot mansion. From these very grounds, laborers mined granite with which to build the home.

*One Prado.
Margaret Mitchell
and husband
John March
lived here.*

In 1925 Ansley's beloved home would become the Governor's Mansion. Goats would graze the lawns of populist Governor Eugene Talmadge; and his son Herman, also to become governor, would milk cows on the outdoor terrace.

The sylvan park became home to the cultured, the wealthy, the mighty, the influential.

Ansley's mansion was one of three to go up in the early stages of the park. Edward Inman built on several lots, and W.F. Winecoff constructed a granite home on a lot that covered an entire block. When fire destroyed Winecoff's home, he erected the exclusive Winecoff Hotel downtown; he and his wife moved into a suite there. John, a son, salvaged granite and marble from the mansion and built his own home that still stands across the street from Jane Harmon's place.

Newspapers around the world headlined the news on December 8, 1946 that, on the night before, fire gutted the Winecoff Hotel, taking a hundred and nineteen lives. Among them were the elder Winecoffs.

Building continued until the early thirties, and the sylvan park became home to the cultured, the wealthy, the mighty, the influential. Atlanta's most noted architects – Neel Reid, Philip Shutze, Thornton Marye, Walter Downing, and Haralson Bleckley among them – finished shaping Edwin Ansley's dream.

It was here that Margaret Mitchell, the petite and diffident author of *Gone with the Wind,* came to live. Never comfortable with fame and wealth, she shared an unpretentious apartment with husband John March at a place now known as One Prado.

Other illustrious residents, though lesser lights than Margaret Mitchell, included the aging Lovick Thomas, a Confederate colonel who distinguished himself against General Sherman's conquering forces in the Battle of Atlanta; Dorothy Alexander, an innovator in ballet, who shared Dance Magazine awards in 1960 with George Balanchine and Fred Astaire; and Michael Hoke an orthopedic physician, who moved from his Tudor home on Peachtree Circle to live in Warm Springs. There he could better treat his famous patient, Franklin D. Roosevelt.

For twenty years Jane Harmon has lived in Ansley Park – a "weathered place" where she feels she can walk alone at night to a neighbor's house. "It's comfortable here," she says. "The feeling comes to you when you drive into the neighborhood."

51 Lafayette Drive. "Flomar", 1935-1985. "Sandcastle", 1985 - present.

Brookwood Hills

*It is
remindful
of the modest
hero who
returns in
splendor, telling
nothing of
past turmoil.*

At the very point where Peachtree Street ends and Peachtree Road begins, landscaped islands separate Brookwood Hills from the bustle of Atlanta. Beyond the gateways of Brighton or Palisades, the clamor of the city fades; roads meander past elegant homes and serene landscapes. There is order, privacy, and peace on this gentle roll of land that calls to mind nothing of rooted anxieties. It is remindful of the modest hero who returns in splendor, telling nothing of past turmoil.

But Elaine Luxemburger and her attorney husband Jerry are among neighbors that tell you that the history of Brookwood Hills has been one battle after another. Nothing, they say, is taken for granted, and wars have steeled neighbors into a formidable force, hammering out long-standing alliances.

"It is a place with its dukes up," says Elaine. "We never let down our guard."

Either by diplomacy or combat, neighbors fend off threats: unwanted development, proposed thoroughfares, invasive crime. In concert they raise money and doughtily approach City Hall or even go to court. They are quick to circle their wagons.

There is strength and confidence in their muster. When the prestigious

*14 Palisades Road
and garden.
The Logan Clark/
Luxemburger Home,
designed by
Neel Reid.*

26

*116
Huntington*

Buckhead Coalition put up signs on Peachtree that told travelers, "You Are Entering Buckhead," residents of Brookwood Hills complained: "Buckhead is a beautiful place, but we're south of Buckhead. Take down the signs."

The signs came down.

Such fortress mentality does not exist in just any neighborhood, but in Brookwood Hills there is a popular meeting place. The forum where most issues are aired is around The Pool, actually a center for recreation and other club activities. Set in a forest glen that at one time was a gully with a natural spring, the center was established by B. F. Burdett, the original developer. Over the years it was a gathering place for people of the city. Many still say, "I know Brookwood; it's where I met my wife," or "where I courted," or "where I went to dances."

In the mid-sixties Elaine Luxemburger brought her young ones from Garden Hills to swim every summer day. Besides the pool and the club, there was a baseball field, a tennis court, swings and a play area. Brookwood Hills began to seem home to the Luxemburgers; in 1968 they bought the Neel Reid-designed home at 14 Palisades Road, and reared their children there.

"Buckhead is a beautiful place, but we're south of Buckhead. Take down the signs."

*200
Camden Road*

Though it lies just off Atlanta's most famous thoroughfare, Brookwood Hills is private and quiet; it feels and looks like a sanctuary. Its avenues curve naturally around wooded hills; its yards flow park-like into one another. Grounds are shaded by towering trees and covered by grasses and shrubbery. In the semi-tropical spring, mockingbirds and wrens recall the Old South, but the real flavor of Brookwood Hills is of the twenties when homes of many styles were built – Tudor, Mediterranean, Neoclassical, Colonial, and Craftsman Bungalow.

A locale of few intrusions or changes, it is now listed on the National Register of Historic Places.

The pool.
A favorite spot
for airing
neighborhood issues.

100
Palisades

36
Wakefield

Cabbagetown

**They hurled
and dodged
rocks; they
called the
locals "cabbage
heads."**

*Berean
Street*

Mary Bankester is a working woman who could choose among a lot of neighborhoods; but Cabbagetown is the place of her fancy. Like a neighbor on the next block, Mary thinks one either loves or hates Cabbagetown. She loves it; the neighbor, who drops by to offer pizza, says he hates it. Later, however, when the neighbor speaks of Cabbagetown, hate is not there.

"You have family here," he says. "You watch the kids grow up and you walk around barefooted; ride your bicycle. You can even sleep outdoors in the garden; nobody's going to bother you."

*Storytelling
on Halloween
afternoon*

To many who have migrated to this old settlement, simplicity is Cabbagetown's charm – different, tranquil, at times beguiling. Although the downtown skyline looms just a mile distant, Atlanta seems far away.

Life here has been uncomplicated since 1881. That was when George Adair gave the area his daughter's name, calling it Pearl Park. In the new century the name changed. When the old Atlanta Crackers played off Ponce de Leon, fans walked miles to the baseball field. Young men from South Atlanta trudged the railroad tracks and often paused to swap insults with boys of the settlement. They hurled and dodged rocks; they called the locals "cabbage heads."

Years before, a cotton mill crowded into Pearl Park. As was the trend, mill officials built homes for the workers. Dwellers of every four houses shared a pump. When piped water finally came, tenants enclosed part of their back porches to house their toilets.

At the most, a third of Cabbagetown's people worked in textiles. Others caned chairs, built furniture, ran butcher shops, or operated grocery marts. Store fronts are still visible on some houses.

As customs changed, the mill found worker housing no longer needed. World War II came and the owners wanted more factory space. They razed dwellings and erected concrete buildings on the vacated land. There they made military uniforms and blankets.

In the fifties the owners sold the plants, but the new operators failed to upgrade machinery and they finally declared bankruptcy. Many Cabbagetown houses were sold from the courthouse steps.

In the sixties, the proud but downgraded neighborhoods of Midtown, Inman Park, Virginia-Highland, and Grant Park began to revive, to gentrify. An influx of new wealth displaced apartment renters, who then looked around for houses they could afford. Many found a haven in Cabbagetown.

Top:
Miz Rhodes Store

Below: 190 Powell

In the nineties, some renters again cried "displacement" as buyers like Mary Bankester discovered bargain homes and renovated them.

Mary found the village when, working with the YWCA, she helped women make and sell quilts. She fashioned a showplace of her first home at Savannah and Tennelle streets. She liked the simplicity, the quietness, the roses that climbed along the Sears-Roebuck chain-link fences. On her first Halloween there she was hooked:

***"There was
a big rabbit,
a man on stilts,
and a woman
in a black
cat costume."***

"I ran to the porch when I heard the racket: boom, boom, tootely, toot. Down the street came people playing all sorts of musical instruments. An awful sound. There was a big rabbit, a man on stilts, and a woman in a black cat costume. Turns out it was Kelly's Feed and Seed Abominable Marching Band. The next year we asked them to come back; we invited people from downtown; we all got out there and marched.

"We call each other by first names. I call it 'street socialization.' If I don't see my neighbor go to work in the morning, I check on her. Neighbors here look out for one another."

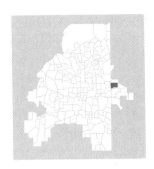

Candler Park

Along the north edge of the old suburb, an abandoned concrete-and-steel pylon hovers over a low greensward like a Stonehenge pillar. It is a dark reminder of dreams that failed in conflict with other dreams.

The area was named for Asa Candler who deeded land there for recreation. In earlier days it had been part of Edgewood, an independent town that sprang up along the tracks of the Georgia Railroad. Besides its train station, Edgewood had two streetcar lines that gave it the character of a commuter town. Then, north of the tracks, Candler Park

McLendon Avenue

came into being. The growing use of the automobile made it attractive to professionals and merchants, who on weekdays drove to work in downtown Atlanta, only three or four miles away.

Many decades later, Atlanta's leaders envisioned a beltway that would lessen the flow of traffic on the city's streets. They planned and launched

361
Oakdale

work on a multilane ribbon that they named the Presidential Parkway.

It was only after officials obtained right-of-ways and began construction that owners along the swath fully understood the impact to their homes.

As grading tore through borders – and as great monoliths rose in Candler Park, Druid Hills, Virginia-Highland, and other such northeastern areas – residents united to protect their personal wealth and the equity of work done to revitalize the neighborhoods.

Candler Park links

When the citizens finally prevailed, Candler Park landowners re-posted "for sale" signs along the right-of-ways. During the crisis they had reasoned that if there was going to be an expressway, they would not easily sell lots and houses there.

Young residents resumed work on the homes and grounds. They golfed on the nine-hole course and their children played in the two parks as before. Candler Park took on fresh life. Though it once faded into a shabby ghost of its former days, its late Victorian, Greek Revival, Tudor, and Craftsman homes now began to take on the look of the practical and lovely neighborhood it used to be.

366
Oakdale

Cascade Heights

*3147
Cascade Drive*

*Mary and
Pelham Williams*

Carved out of towering pine forests just a few decades ago, the neighborhood today is home to more middle-class black Americans than any other place in Georgia. It seems disembodied from Atlanta, its generous triangular boundaries stretching from the Perimeter superhighway in the southwest, and pointing east to the city's underbelly.

Illustrious citizens have resided in the handsome environment of Cascades Heights: Maynard Jackson lived here during his first term as mayor; Andrew Young, former United Nations ambassador and recent mayor, still has a home here, as does the Rev. Joseph E. Lowery, chairman of the internationally known Southern Christian Leadership Conference.

There is no other place like it in Atlanta. Its rolling hills, pine forests, tumbling cascades, winding roads, and placid valleys seem a world

*Kingsdale
Avenue*

**Its rolling hills,
pine forests,
tumbling cascades,
winding roads,
and placid
valleys seem
a world apart.**

apart. Indeed, this feeling of difference brought affluent blacks to the neighborhood in the sixties, and they eventually outnumbered their white neighbors by three to one.

■ ■ ■

In the living room of their large and quiet ranch home in the pines, Pelham and Mary Williams speak of the neighborhood's greening. They came here in the early seventies, one of the few black families; their neighbors were friendly but distant. Pelham has since resigned from his commissioner's job with the city to open a consulting engineering firm; the Williams children are now gone from Cascade Heights.

Their offspring wanted to come back to the place they avowedly loved, but like other young ones who once lived here, they could not afford the prices of homes.

*"Developers
had ideas –
some good,
some bad –
and these ideas
brought us
together."*

*Magnum
Lane*

"This was farmland before the early thirties," says Pelham. "But a number of subdivisions spawned up around Atlanta and this was among them. We've watched it grow, and we've come to know many white owners who chose to stay and help develop the community."

Now teachers, ministers, doctors, lawyers, and business people live in Cascade Heights. Including neighbors in surrounding communities, there are about three hundred families working together in the Neighborhood Planning Unit.

"There are a series of catalysts that keep us together," says Pelham. "When we first moved out here, you'd see people in their yards and wave to them, but that was about it."

Inevitably, trouble came, and the Williamses were delighted to find themselves soon surrounded with a league of allies.

"First there were the problems of zoning," Pelham explains. "Developers had ideas – some good, some bad – and these ideas brought us together. We expressed our concerns. We let it be known that new developments had to conform to the desires of the community; also, they had to meet zoning requirements."

Neighbors tightened their bonds when it became apparent that petty criminals had found the remote Cascade Heights an easy target.

"We all became involved in crime-watch programs," says Pelham. "The distance between us became shorter with the zoning issues, but the neighborhood watch program clapped us together in a tight unit. Now, within this NPU, we've at last come together socially."

Mary Williams is now in a kind of ad hoc committee that takes up various concerns of all neighborhoods within the planning unit – concerns such as city services, public safety, and zoning.

"That's what a community should be," she says. "There are a number of new subdivisions being built; so there is an encouragement to define our boundaries so we can be alert against crime. On a daily basis, we need to know who's watching out for who."

Neighbors, who in the early days seemed standoffish, later proved anything but shy. After they found reason to come together, residents took up arms like seasoned combatants; they became comrades both politically and socially. They now know each other so well that almost any one of them can predict the time of day a neighbor will go to the polls in an election. Their average voting turnout is an incredible eighty percent.

Like their counterparts in exclusive white neighborhoods, they defend hearth and home with both money and political force. The defense of their neighborhood is little different from that of well-to-do and wealthy homeowners of any other color.

Neighbors, who in the early days seemed standoffish, later proved anything but shy.

1225 Oakcrest Drive

Druid Hills

It is not just a place to live. Druid Hills is a bold sketch laid upon canvas by a master painter – its pigments and texture changing gently with the times.

In the days before superhighways, travelers heading east or west drove through Druid Hills and marveled at the serpentine Ponce de Leon Avenue. Six linear parks lay in the middle; gracious homes rose before great trees to the sides, and sprawling lawns of homes and lush parks seemed to flow into one another. In many ways the scene is country England, though the manors are of eclectic origin and the great oaks, maples, and magnolias are relics of the Old South.

Above:
Entrance to
Conservation Park

Right:
826 Springdale Road

Druid Hills did not derive from a failed plantation economy. It grew from the restless adventuring of developer Joel Hurt who, like most Atlanta visionaries, put the late war behind him and sought amity and commerce with the South's conquerors.

Early in the Gay Nineties Hurt consulted New Englander Frederick Law Olmsted, the country's foremost landscape architect. He wanted

*948
Lullwater*

The nine-room home at 822 Lullwater Road was the set for the movie Driving Miss Daisy.

his development (not yet called Druid Hills) to bear the flavor of Olmsted's other North American triumphs: Washington's Capitol grounds, New York's Central Park, Chicago's Riverside, Montreal's Royal Park.

Olmsted, an avowed opponent of slavery, had come south before the war to report weekly to the editor of the *New York Times* on the workings of a slave economy. After the war the noted humanitarian apparently

A linear park along Ponce de Leon Avenue

bore no grudge against the southern people. Writing to his stepson from the Vanderbilt Estate in North Carolina where he designed the grounds, he observed that, "Very soon our northern cities will have been provided with parks. I am moved by a desire to get a footing at the South."

Olmsted designed preliminary plans for Druid Hills in 1893, but ill health caused him to retire two years later. It was left to his sons Frederick, Jr. and John Charles to complete the project. They worked faithfully to achieve their father's concepts of beauty, to preserve aesthetics that had already changed the face of other important cities.

Joel Hurt sold his interest in the development in 1908, and Forrest Adair told the *Atlanta Journal* that the buyers would "further carry out the plans originally suggested by Mr. Olmsted."

From that time until World War II, Druid Hills flowered into a fairyland. Its homes sat upon spacious grounds that reflected Olmsted's vision. The grace and elegance of Ponce de Leon Avenue soon spilled over into other tree-lined residential areas of Atlanta.

Lullwater Road

After World War II times changed. From the languid pace of a charming old southern city, Atlanta burgeoned into a major American metropolis. The movers and shakers of the first half of the century had grown older and many were dying. Executors sold off the old estates and standards began to fall. Owners who stayed often could not pay the high price of upkeep.

The deterioration was not confined to Atlanta. In the fashionable country club areas throughout America – Beverly Hills, Mission Hills, Forest

Park, the Hamptons, and Newport among them – grand mansions began to lose their luster. For two decades many of Druid Hills's stately homes grew dowdy: shrubbery wilted, lawns grew over, and great oaks and maples languished unpruned. Not until the seventies did gradual rebirth begin, and it still goes on.

Newcomers and scions of old families have come together to salvage old Druid Hills. Multifamily buildings dot the landscape, but the charm of earlier days still peeks through. An expressway was begun but the outcry of the community stopped it. The lawns of the parks along Ponce de Leon show bald, red-clay spots, but money was gathered for a master plan to restore the parks to the grand dream of Frederick Olmsted. A national historic designation, severely restricting sub-standard development, is the current hope of the neighborhood groups.

Through the ups and downs of Druid Hills, Emory University's pastoral campus has been a steadying anchor, and along the corridor there are beautiful churches and museums. Ponce de Leon Avenue fortunately is no longer a major thoroughfare, but it remains a rare jewel and was designated the official eastern route for the 1996 Olympics.

St. John Chrysoston Melkite Church, former home of Coca-Cola founder Asa Candler.

41

Garden Hills

They met in law school, married, and moved to Atlanta. Then while renting a house on Habersham Road, Laurie and Kirven Gilbert looked for a place to settle and rear a family. They wanted to experience the city, yet to live in the way they grew up – she in Virginia, he in Georgia. They wanted a community feel: parks, pools, sidewalks, families, schools. At first they looked outside the I-285 flange where doctors and lawyers live next door to top corporate executives. Nice. But not for the Gilberts.

"Homeowners outside I-285 have up-to-date, spacious places," says Laurie. "Yet, most come from other regions and do not connect with Atlanta. They don't know the city, never feel they meet people from the city."

In the mid-twenties, attorney P.C. McDuffie developed Garden Hills to be a town within a city. Shops and stores were scattered along Peachtree. Two schools came to be within the neighborhood, and

*371
Pinehills Road*

churches dotted the nearby landscape. As Atlanta spread, more than a hundred shops were in place nearby when the Gilberts in 1984 bought and settled into a Dutch Colonial that architects Smith & Downing designed nearly sixty years before.

182
Rumson

Laurie Gilbert

McDuffie was ahead of his time. Although he initiated his project on rolling forest acres and laid it out to conform with Frederick Olmsted's now-prevailing landscape pattern, he also planned for urban living in a rural-like environment. Besides causing two schools to be built in the neighborhood, and besides locating near shops and stores, McDuffie provided for multifamily housing, not just single-family homes. In wooded dales he laid out playgrounds. Day-to-day conveniences were put at the fingertips of homeowners, and downtown Atlanta was only minutes away.

The styles range widely. There are one- and two-story homes on one-third acre lots: Tudor, English Cottage, American Colonial, Dutch Colonial, Georgian, and even Moorish and French. All houses are constructed solidly – a prime requirement in the Gilberts' choosing a home here.

Garden Hills has always been a "down-home" neighborhood – houses maintained and yards kept up. Although it is a scenic neighborhood, the atmosphere is not that of the home-and-garden magazines. Rather, it is a place where children play and residents putter about the grounds.

Says Laurie: "When visitors think of the Tuxedo Park and Peachtree Battle areas, they think of manors and gorgeous, manicured lawns. When they drive through Garden Hills they don't have that same feeling. The yards are more informal and there may be autumn leaves on the ground. This is more like a place one would grow up in. Lots of big trees for climbing, neat houses, all different. You are not in a showplace, nor are you in a sub-division where houses look the same, just painted different colors. You feel that these houses are substantial, that they've been here a long time, that they'll be here a hundred years from now."

2870 North Hills Road

Laurie and Kirven bought their home when they had no children; now they have two. Most homeowners around them are of a similar age, have children, and work to maintain and improve the neighborhood. There are fund-raisings to keep up the parks – Easter egg hunts, Halloween and Christmas parties. There is an old-time neighborhood feeling that is precious to those who live here. As families grow, owners simply add to their homes.

*Recreation
Center Pool*

*Annual
Christmas Party*

*Garden Hills
Elementary
School*

"This could be the only house we'll ever have," says Laurie. "We came here to start a family, and our children someday may bring their children to visit. You get entrenched with your neighbors, and it's not easy to think of moving and changing your locale."

Grant Park

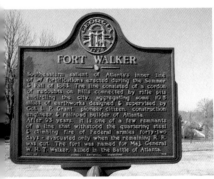

Velocipedes and horse cars coursed these shaded streets a hundred years ago. They traveled past the Victorian homes that sprang up in the aftermath of the Civil War. To the center of the neighborhood, excursionists came with parasols to glide in boats upon the lake, to see exotic animals, to spread picnics upon the green, and to lounge and frolic in the famous park that gave the place its name. Indeed, in the Gay Nineties, Grant Park was remindful of the Parisian playgrounds of Renoir paintings; it called to mind the celebrated parks of Geneva, San Francisco, Niagara, Rome, and London. By the turn of the century it was a holiday mecca for all of the South.

Ruins of the
Grant Mansion
on St. Paul
Street

Lemuel Grant's antebellum mansion decays amid live oaks and overgrown weeds.

Colonel L.P. Grant

Facing page:
Atlanta
skyline from
Fort Walker

The park and neighborhood rose upon land once owned by Lemuel P. Grant, a New England engineer who arrived in 1850 to help build railroads. When war loomed, Grant became a colonel in the Confederate militia and was charged with building Atlanta's defenses. With the help of slaves from North Georgia plantations, he encircled the city with seventeen redoubts. One stronghold was erected upon his own land, upon a ridge overlooking the city. Today an outline of the old fort swells from a grassy bluff at the southeast corner of the park. Standing here, one may see on the north horizon a tall and brilliant skyline radiating miles from old Five Points.

Thirty years after he built the bulwarks, Colonel Grant donated eighty-five acres of this land for a park. His gift prohibited no race or class of people; the grounds were open to everyone. The city government added more acres, and lumberman George Gress bought a defunct circus to populate a zoo; Gress also obtained the much-traveled 50-by-400-foot painting of the Battle of Atlanta, and displayed it permanently. In 1921 this 18,000-pound work of twelve German artists was taken from its old wooden structure and housed in a new marble building. Already the great canvas had become widely known as the Cyclorama.

By the 1900s, middle-class and upper middle-class families had built generously around the park. The neighborhood flourished until mid-century when its third and fourth generations began to leave for the suburbs. In the 1960s, an east-west interstate highway cut through the area just south of Oakland Cemetery. Year by year, the proud park withered; old-timers reluctantly wrote it off as a shabby relic.

47

In the 1970s young buyers – sensing unusual values in the rundown Victorian homes – infiltrated the old area. No other part of the city yielded such choices of nineteenth-century treasures. Whites, blacks, and hispanics arrived in equal numbers over the next two decades. Most of them bought homes; they painted and repaired them; they formed neighborhood units and won a national register district status. Annually since 1973 visitors come from all over Atlanta to tour the selected homes, to see which places have taken on new life.

Probably beyond repair, Lemuel Grant's antebellum mansion decays amid live oaks and overgrown weeds. But in the pastel-painted homes scattered around it, there are recurrent dreams of a neighborhood revival.

Orleans and Broyles Street

Glen Castle on Glenwood Avenue

Retracing the horse car routes of a century ago, one may see proud Victorian homes in their old splendor. The homes are mauve and aqua, olive and peach, dark green and white, terra-cotta and turquoise green. The lively colors temper the imposing embroidery of ancient dwellings.

▪ ▪ ▪

As clouds threaten on a Sunday morning, a flaxen-headed, brightly dressed child unfurls a toy umbrella and runs from the church to her mother. A whistling black boy, arms folded, pedals a pink-painted spider bicycle along Cherokee Avenue. On the heights of the park, children of light, dark, and sepia skins play upon the relics of Lemuel Grant's redoubts.

*Atlanta Jazz
Festival in
Grant Park*

Inman Park

Many think it was civil engineer Joel Hurt – not the notable architects of the early century – who most influenced the beauty of Atlanta.

Even before he summoned the great landscaper Frederick Law Olmsted to design the linear parks of Druid Hills, Hurt developed Inman Park as the city's first planned garden suburb. He envisioned the Olmsted plan of Chicago's Riverside as the way the development should look, and he backed his image of the ideal with his own fortune.

It was upon farmland east of downtown that Hurt established Inman

105
David Circle

Park. In 1887 he employed James Forsyth Johnson to design the landscape in the manner of Olmsted. He brought in live oak trees from coastal Georgia and – even though such plants had not been known to survive before in Atlanta's climate – they have shaded Inman Park for a century.

The Great Depression of 1893 slowed progress, but Hurt continued his plan. He moved to Inman Park to be near the development. Soon other prominent Atlantans began to move out from the city and to build great homes there. In 1902, Asa Candler, founder of the Coca-Cola Company, built his Callan Castle; Ernest Woodruff, a top executive with the firm, also came. Other notables included George King, Robert Winship, and Wilbur Fiske.

In the first decade of the new century, Inman Park enjoyed its epoch of

*Inman Park
Spring Festival*

*Joel Hurt home.
167 Elizabeth Street
circa 1905*

glory. Joel Hurt planned and engineered the city's first electric trolley line; it began downtown and ended at the shingled, High Victorian car barn that still stands on Edgewood Avenue. Earlier, and farther down the street, Hurt built the city's first skyscraper. The large residential lots he laid out were soon the sites of magnificent homes – Classical Revival, Queen Anne High Victorian, and Late Victorian. Near these were ten acres of Springvale Park and Crystal Lake.

Having already influenced the style and growth of Atlanta, Hurt turned to develop prestigious Druid Hills. At the same time, Ansley Park, another classic suburb, was being built, and Atlanta's elite became interested in both. By 1910 Inman Park had lost many of its wealthiest homeowners to the new and more contemporary suburbs. But even though Joel Hurt made neighboring Druid Hills one of America's most admired garden places, he remained in Inman Park until he died in 1927.

Over the next half century, Inman Park declined. Small houses sprang up on the parklike Mesa, hords of renters came in during World War II, and cheap apartments began to clutter the scene. The glow of proud old homes dimmed, yards and parks withered; by the sixties, this proud old suburb – Atlanta's grand dame from Victorian times – was considered by many to be a slum.

It was on a dreary wet day in 1969 that Robert Griggs rode through the gloom of Inman Park and spotted a bedraggled Queen Anne-style

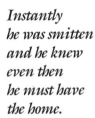

*Instantly
he was smitten
and he knew
even then
he must have
the home.*

*Beath-Griggs Home
860 Euclid Avenue*

52

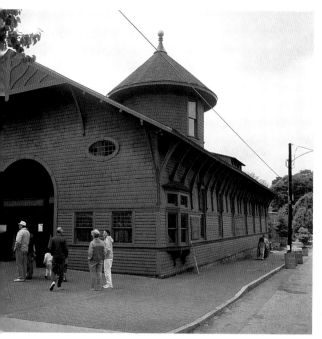

The trolley barn on Edgewood Avenue, now and then.

Victorian house. Instantly he was smitten and knew even then that he must have the home. It was from this point that the revival of Inman Park began.

Others soon dared to reclaim homes of the run-down neighborhood, and they formed Inman Park Restoration, Inc., the city's first civic association. When more than a hundred homes were demolished in the path of I-485, neighbors joined to help kill the highway.

The Inman Park Spring Festival has for more than two decades brought people from Atlanta and places beyond. Visitors with similar associations in San Francisco, Philadelphia, Savannah, Raleigh, and Macon have come to Inman Park to trade ideas. No longer do Atlantans think of it as a tired old relic.

Today, butterfly designs hang from windows and walls of homes. They denote a transformation of ugliness to loveliness. A profile on each wing looks outward. The two faces represent Janus, an ancient Roman diety who kept the gate of Heaven. Residents say he looks to the past and the future at the same time.

Asa Candler Home circa 1902-03

Right: 192 Hurt Street

At the Crossroads

Lakewood Heights

It is a pleasant Sunday morning in late summer. In the village center, where Lakewood Avenue and Jonesboro Road cross to make an X, streets and sidewalks are empty and bars and stores closed. Saturday night carousers and streetwalkers left in the early hours.

Vehicles line the curbs several blocks down the avenue, and from within a tidily kept church comes the muffled sound of offertory singing. Soon a side door swings open and a man in his sixties steps into the sunlight. He will wait for ushers to bring the morning's proceeds for his accounting.

Lakewood Drive and Jonesboro Road

"No, I don't live around here," he says. "Used to, but I moved out long ago; moved down near Locust Grove. Hated to leave here...a good place to grow up; but I only come back to go to church. The bad elements, you know; too many transients, people who don't want to get along with others; too many robberies, too much crime."

Yet, another man who has lived down Jonesboro Road for forty years says crime seems to be no different in Lakewood Heights than anywhere else.

"Maybe we all see things differently," he says.

Motorcyclist Bill Kraus, a transplanted resident who says he has three graduate degrees ("... including a doctor of divinity in Zen Bhuddist philosophy"), takes whatever comes. He is a spokesman in matters affecting the community, and he likes Lakewood Heights as it is ("excellent values") and for what it could become:

"We're trying to recreate the sense of an urban village where people walk past and smile, where they work together at the Mindis plant and shops and stores. We've got the Cadillac of boys clubs here, and other elements show real promise."

Kraus is a formidable man who smiles often and trusts easily. But his large and restless dogs and the hand-printed warning sign out front hint of limits to his good nature. He works off and on "in the millwork line" but expects soon to return to the corrections field. Atlanta's Federal Prison is just outside his neighborhood.

Fifty years ago, Lakewood Heights was a busy community made up mostly of General Motors plant workers. The village's retail competition was more than five miles away in Atlanta's downtown. Stores and shops drew neighbors from other areas – among them, Orchard Park, Polar Rock, Benteen, Chosewood Park, Thomasville, Clark University, and Gammon Theological Seminary. Starting in 1901 a trolley line ran from the village down to Lakewood Park, and people came from all of Georgia to visit the fair nearby.

Lakewood Heights intersection, 1928.

The fall of the proud village came when General Motors closed its doors and the colleges moved to the Atlanta University campus. Public housing renters moved in when students and faculty left to go with Clark University. The neighborhood disintegrated. Only since the Mindis recycling plant moved into the vacated General Motors building has Lakewood Heights begun its slow rebound. Two small plants have joined Mindis.

"The idea is to get back to what Lakewood Heights used to be," says Bill Kraus. "Let's rebuild some of these downtrodden homes; let's walk around with our heads held high again."

On his Harley-Davidson, Kraus rides into Atlanta and takes the neighborhood's case to City Hall.

"They hate me," says a grinning Kraus. "I don't ever come offering anything."

Kraus and his neighbors are feisty. They blocked attempts to open two junkyards, and they stopped a concrete recycling plant from coming in.

"Let's rebuild some of these downtrodden homes; let's walk around with our heads held high again."

Bill Kraus

"Those who love this place are blue-collar people," Kraus says. "They've got that puritan mentality. Bikers ride Harleys; others buy Chevrolet pickups. It's 'Yea, America!,' and the people deplore imports."

Up where Jonesboro and Lakewood intersect, a tax accountant shows an old photograph of the crossroads. The village is easily recognizable in its picture of sixty-five years ago. The man seems unaffected by the changes wrought by passing years. He is proud and hopeful and says he manages a good living here.

78
Claire Street

1827
Lakewood Terrace

Midtown

In the late fifties the district interlacing the northern edge of downtown Atlanta fell upon hard times. Scions of old families moved away and in their wake transients moved in – tough biker gangs, ne'er-do-wells, ladies with painted faces. Old cars rusted on weed-covered grounds. Frequently trouble came, and police called it a tenderloin area.

It was amid this decay that up-and-coming architect Henri Jova searched for a duplex to buy. Jova, a world traveler, had arrived from Manhattan four years before and lived alone in a northside carriage house; he called it "a fingerbowl neighborhood." Already the Cornell graduate had won

*865
Mentelle Drive*

the Rome Prize and had been a Fulbright fellow. He was yet to design Colony Square, but his other credentials – his paintings and interior designs – impressed Atlantans. Now his landlord relatives were giving notice: they were moving, and Henri's cottage was being sold along with their home. Jova then looked for a simple house, one that had not been refinished. He did not want to pay for improvements other people had made.

A perplexed broker took Jova to the kind of place he seemed to want.

Built in 1929, the palatial Fox Theatre was saved from the wrecking ball in recent years.

760 Myrtle Street

It was from this moment that the strange odyssey of Midtown's revival began.

"A ratty and impossible old duplex," friends told Henri, "...a dwelling you're sure to find distasteful."

"Well," said Jova after inspecting its structure, "I kind of like it." It was from this moment that the strange odyssey of Midtown's revival began.

For more than a decade, Henri Jova lived in the downstairs part of the duplex he renovated. People told Henri that his old friends would not visit him, would not come to his parties. But soon they did begin to come; they shared parking with pickup trucks and motorcycles of the neighborhood.

Jova bought two adjoining lots and built a townhouse for his parents. When he took drawings downtown to obtain a building permit, engineers from back offices sauntered in. They wanted to see the man who was planning the first single-family residence since World War II to be built in this nest of seething penury. They were astonished by the small but grand design that would include an elevator.

59

The loose morals flaunted along Seventh Street offended his mother, so Henri bought every house and apartment building from Charles Allen Drive to Mentelle Drive. It was the first step in ridding the place of its lowlife. He redesigned the vacated buildings and brought in young neighbors who wished to live in the city and to share in Midtown's renewal.

Before its Jovian renaissance Midtown had no name.

Before its Jovian renaissance Midtown had no name; nevertheless, as artists, landscape architects, newspaper executives, students, and young career people began to move in, real estate prices steadily climbed. Neighbors bound themselves into a civic unit and together settled issues at City Hall. Today Midtown is a mix of wealthy, comfortable, and poor – not unlike the intown life of New York or London.

Jova was called a maverick when he revived Midtown's residential area and later when he built a showplace home on Mentelle Drive. He became an absolute iconoclast when he designed the massive Colony Square high-rise project in the lethargic business area of Midtown. He was deeply involved, and the complex at first seemed to fail – but finally it boomed and the creative Jova enjoyed the praise that followed. His work propagated the rise of other skyscrapers along the Midtown area of Peachtree Street.

*Left:
417 5th Street*

*Right:
857 Durant Street*

*The
Georgian Terrace
Hotel*

*Home of
Henry Jova.
861 Mentelle Drive.*

*"I want to
live where I
can see the
skyline."*

Lynn Meyer and Beth Ruddiman found Midtown soon after college. They came so they could be near their volunteer work and the city's centers of art. They feel lucky to have been among the discoverers, but say people just out of college would find it hard to afford today's prices.

In the spirit of Henri Jova they helped improve the neighborhood. "When you start living amid old surroundings," says Lynn, "you realize how much work is involved. You never finish."

Both young women are now addicted to downtown living. Beth says that to really appreciate it, one should walk around the neighborhood. Lynn says she runs in Piedmont Park in late afternoons as long as there is daylight. "When I first moved here I could look over and see the Fox [the preserved classic theatre], and the belvederes on Ponce de Leon. I can always see the skyline here. There's something about the intown thing I like. I want to live where I can see the skyline."

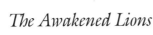

Morningside-Lenox Park

The communities were separate until The Highway threatened. But in the sixties, when wrecking balls began knocking down houses, neighbors of Morningside Park and Lenox Park came together. With other eastern Atlanta groups they stopped construction of I-485 – only the second time such a thing ever happened.

That was in 1973. Today, residents regard the swath of ruins as a reminder to keep watch always.

One schoolboy thinks the idea works too well. On a day he played hookey, he was no more than two minutes from Morningside Elementary when his mother took three calls from neighbors. Ruefully the boy acknowledged: "A kid can't get away with nothin' around here."

1798
Windmere

In 1923, developers promoted the area as "the realm of beauty." They planned it on land close by the campus of Lanier University, founded by a Baptist minister in 1917. The clergyman envisioned buildings to represent mansions of the South, but he succeeded in erecting only one – a replica of the Custis-Lee mansion. When the school failed, ironically the Ku Klux Klan bought it; a year later they sold it to Jewish residents who established Shearith Israel Synagogue there. The mansion still stands and the synagogue survives despite the loss of many old Jewish neighbors.

A six-classroom school opened in 1928, and seven years later government workers completed the present Morningside Elementary building. Penmanship, poetry, and literary work were emphasized, and the school flourished. But when integration came, many neighborhood children were sent to private schools.

One mother regrets now that she did not do enough to help the school in its travail: "Many of us cannot say we jumped in and supported the public school. Those were difficult times, and we sent our children to private schools at first to spare them the upheaval. But today integration has been long accepted."

Minorities today make up but a small segment of the school, even while public schools in the rest of the city are heavily black and hispanic.

Morningside is a popular school. It is also a shelter for children of the homeless. A neighbor explains:

"Children come to the school in transit. "They stay for no more than

Below and right: Celebration of summer in the sunken garden

Above: Morningside Elementary School

63

thirty days. Right away we give them a backpack of supplies; when they walk in on that first day they look like any other student. They don't want to stand out, and everybody respects that. Regulars at the school sense the differences, but they never ask why the children come and go. They try to make the transients feel at home."

Morningside/Lenox Park people are proud of their community's makeup. "We have Jews, gentiles, gays, blacks, singles, mixed-marrieds," says a neighbor, "...anyone who wants to live here and can afford it. And there are few multifamily buildings."

The
neighborhood
is run like
a marblecake
government.

The neighborhood is run like a marblecake government, its issues swirling down and back from top committees to households. Residents understand that the city cannot give all the protection and services they need, so they help themselves. They understand the power of coming together to fight laws and ordinances they deem unfair or to pressure developers into preserving the neighborhood.

1752
North Pelham

Fourteen committees flourish. They oversee such activities as parks, public safety, senior services, home tours, beautification, zoning efforts, education, and historic preservation.

Every year there are Halloween parties in Noble Park, Easter egg hunts in Sydney Marcus Park, and a celebration of summer in a garden area known as the Rose Bowl.

There are more parks divided among neighbors here than in any other section in Atlanta. When one asks homeowners to describe their neighborhood, they may begin by telling of the school, the green spaces, the homes and grounds, and the brick gates they built to mark their borders.

Mozley Park

As General Sherman surrounded Confederate Atlanta in the early summer of 1864, the war was winding down. Yet, Sherman had been instructed to lay waste to the city, a chore that he accepted seriously. By July 28, he had set up two formidable positions southwest of town near Ezra Church. General Hood brought his Southern forces out to meet Sherman, and a short battle followed: It was one of the most one-sided losses the Confederates suffered in the war. Hood counted five thousand casualties; Sherman only six hundred. But the battle indicated to the Northern general that winning Atlanta would mean enormous casualties unless he brought in siege guns from Chattanooga. Thus, the Battle of Ezra Church–on the playground of today's Mozley Park – helped early on to determine the bombardment and destruction of Atlanta.

After the war, a Confederate soldier named Hiram Mozley settled the area now known as Battle Hill. The property was part of his family's estate. He became a physician and invented a popular patent medicine that he called Mozley's Lemon Elixir. When he died, his estate was sold for a subdivision.

Thirty-one years after the Battle of Ezra Church, the surrounding land – now dotted with small homes–was incorporated into the city; it was called Mozley Park. The development grew slowly from east to west around the park. The lots were small, and there were no driveways because automobiles were scarce. Residents rode trolleys to shop and work downtown. White children played in the park.

1487
Martin Luther King
Boulevard

More than a hundred of them descended upon the state capitol and the mayor's office.

Lena Street

After the second World War, Negro soldiers returned home to marry and rear families. They argued that they had fought for their country and had already mingled as equals with other races; they had difficulty coming to terms with segregation at home.

In 1949 a black clergyman named W. W. Witherspool brought his family to live in Mozley Park. His arrival quickly created tension among neighbors. More than a hundred of them descended upon the state capitol and the mayor's office. Among their concerns were the deterioration of the neighborhood and the decline of house values. What followed was the development of a dialogue between white and black leaders. The color line broke, and in the years to come, as black people moved in, white people moved out.

1365
Mozley Place

By 1958 Mozley Park was largely inhabited by minorities, and that is the year that Dr. W.E. Wilson brought his wife and young son to live at the brick bungalow he had built near the park on the north edge of the neighborhood. He was surrounded by people of his own race, middle-class people who bought older homes or built homes in the few vacant spaces left.

Today the neighborhood is greying. Many residents, including Wilson's wife and son, have died. Now retired, the aging doctor lives alone.

*"You want to
get them upset,
do something
negative to the
neighborhood."*

"It is a good, stable neighborhood," he says. "It is restful, convenient, and relatively safe. I don't think I would want to live anywhere else."

He says that even though some original homeowners are now gone, the homes are mostly occupied, usually by those who inherited them.

"All of them seem concerned. You want to get them upset, do something negative to the neighborhood; you'll hear from them. They want the area kept up; they want it to be safe. You don't find them always running in and out of a neighbor's house, but still they watch out for one another. When a family is away overnight, others look out for their house. There's very little crime here compared to other sections of the city."

Still, the doctor locks the white, ornate iron entry door. Some evenings he joins spectators at the playground across the street. It is there he watches youngsters play games upon the very soil where warriors once battled for their lives.

*The neighborhood
from Mathewson*

*Frank L. Stanton
Elementary School*

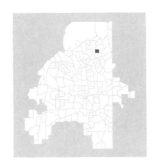

Peachtree Heights

*The
Duck Pond*

When on a June day in 1909, E. Rivers (he preferred "E" to his given name of Eretus) served luncheon on the grounds of his new development off Peachtree Road, two-thousand curious visitors came. Rivers sold eighty-two lots and he was to have other auctions until he sold out the development. Within the year, several houses and apartments were going up on a place that had been woods and farmland. Rivers, a handsome and resolute man, provided the most up-to-date conveniences: piped water, manufactured gas, electric lights, and street cars.

Soon houses of many styles sprinkled the Peachtree Heights landscape. Among them were Colonial Revival, Georgian, Dutch Revival, Greek Revival, Tudor, and Craftsman/Bungalow. The automobile was not

2636
Winslow

*"We
decided
to stay
forever. "*

*Arlene and
Bill Bell*

yet a force, so porte cocheres and detached car sheds were yet to come
about. Construction on E. Rivers lots continued for eighty years, and
today the feeling of the neighborhood is comfortable and the styles
derive from many sources.

Aerospace engineer Bill Bell and his wife Arlene came upon their two-
story Craftsman classic in 1978. The old owner had modernized but did
not tinker with the original 1910 style. Bill himself was handy with tools
but he and Arlene felt they would hold the cards they had been dealt.

"In the spring and fall I come home from work and just sit out there
on the front porch," Bill says. "It's like living in the country: the tall
trees shading the streets and homes, the greens of spring, the varied
colors of fall. Yet we're five minutes away from everything."

When the Bells' second child came, their attachment for the vicinity

2551
Potomac Avenue

("...a place not changed much from the twenties") had become so strong that they improvised for space. "We put down the pros and cons of staying or moving," says Arlene. "Somehow the house became more than a house. We decided to stay forever; we must have known this even when we moved in."

The neighborhood is a mixed advantage to the Bell offspring. The elder son goes to a nearby school with children of thirty nations.

"Our third-grader is better off for this eclectic experience," says Arlene. "He has no idea that his world is different from other people; he has no inkling of prejudice. We're not the only parents with such an experience. A lady with a Ph.D up the street – whose children went all the way through the international school system – feels her now-grown offspring have became critical thinkers. She thinks that might not have developed in an ordinary school."

Nevertheless, Arlene wonders if today's living deprives her young ones of the joy of her own times:

"In Birmingham where I grew up, everybody went to the same school. Here we have Christ the King, a Roman Catholic school, and many in-town private schools. My child lives right across the street from another child he's never played with, not once. The other child is in an after-school program and doesn't get home until after six; they just don't know each other.

"Today we worry about crime. Our children could be going down to the Duck Pond to play by themselves, but occasionally strange people come down there. That is a gnawing concern; I think we worry about them more than our parents had to worry about us."

The neighborhood is made up mostly of white-collar, professional residents. It has been this way generally since E. Rivers broke ground to start the development. Except for a brief period in the sixties when a handful of hippies moved in and lounged about the Duck Pond, there has been little fluctuation in the life styles of people in Peachtree Heights.

Along the Bells' street, there live a physician, an engineer, a stock broker, a health care executive, an investor, and a restaurateur.

There have been a few building encroachments coming from Peachtree Road, but the Bells and their neighbors are vigilant.

"This is a great place to live, and we're trying to preserve its unique historical value and its superb architecture," says Bill Bell.

"Because when it's gone it's gone."

Arlene wonders if today's living deprives her young ones of the joy of her own times.

139 Lakeview

Peachtree Hills

As a boy, Bo Holland lived across the street from the Duck Pond and went to Christ the King School; he liked to stroll through nearby Peachtree Hills, an inviting enclave of modest and start-up homes. But as families grew old, the locale began to lose its luster, and by the time Bo grew up it was a dream in memory only. It ran to seed in the way of most city neighborhoods of the time.

But Bo came to understand the ups and downs of urban real estate. Now in the construction business, he reasoned that since Peachtree Hills was near Atlanta's Midtown but also in the midst of the high-priced neighborhoods of Buckhead, a bit of painting and repairing would make its homes alluring to young marrieds. Moreover, most buyers his age had already missed the years when inflation helped pay for a

*Covenant
Presbyterian
Church.*

***When
Carolyn
was down
with flu,
Dot delivered
hot food to
her door.***

house. So Bo and his wife chose a home in Peachtree Hills. They would fix it up on the logic that maybe a decade later the area would flower. Equity would grow as other young couples discovered the values.

Bo's thinking proved sound. Young and old people alike found good buys; they took their places beside older homeowners who were delighted with the inflow of new energy. A neighborhood association was activated, and soon two small community newspapers were circulating.

Young Susan Conger and her husband joined older residents and further added vitality. And an appreciative Carolyn Cooper remembers

*"Now at
least we have
our day in
court."*

that long-timer Dot Champion lent tools and brought refreshments when Carolyn and her husband prepared to move in. When Carolyn was down with flu, Dot delivered hot food to her door.

Though a total makeover is far from finished, the old section today is a bright and different place. But its dwellers know they must depend mostly upon themselves to make things happen.

Because city leaders must struggle to provide even the scant basics to neighborhoods, residents accept their do-it-yourself status. When an unwanted issue arises, they go to City Hall in phalanx to fight their case.

"Before the neighborhood planning unit system was put in place, we didn't even have a forum," says Bo Holland. "But the mayor is big on neighborhoods. Learning of the problems he and City Hall wrestle with makes us a bit antsy here. We learn of the city's shortfalls and revenue problems. It's a real civics lesson to go down there. Before we became a unit, you had to go fight battles alone against maybe a developer and a high-powered lawyer. Now at least we have our day in court."

*Restaurant in
the King's Circle
Shopping Center*

35
Roanoke Avenue

Pittsburgh

They once played in this very park. Today they come back and spread blankets upon the scraggly lawn. They stand by variegated Arabian tents and greet friends of the old neighborhood. Their locked cars line the curbs of Garibaldi, Windsor, and Delevan streets. They come from places like Cleveland, Detroit, New York City. It is homecoming, and the old neighbors ignore the badly kept homes and the across-the-street parade of drugged wanderers and bold prostitutes.

"Oh, honey, don't pay attention to that," a well-dressed matron tells you. "Look past that...see only the place this used to be."

An outsider looks about but cannot envision Pittsburgh before it turned shoddy. Nevertheless, close by the park, the brick bungalow home of

Below:
Melba Moore
Carter

Right:
McDaniel at
Gardner Street

an old woman shines like a first magnitude star. The iron bars of the doors and windows are white and spotless. The lawn is newly cut, and red and white impatiens speak of unremitting dignity.

After leaving the park, the woman reminisces:"My husband – he's passed on, you know – had a barber shop you could walk to from here. We built this house forty-five years ago, and I've got no plans to leave it."

A couple from New York City drops by. The old woman unlocks the wrought-iron outer door. In a living room adorned with pictures and mementos, the woman presides. She talks of her young days. The visitors grew up in the Pittsburgh section after the woman and her husband built the house; and today they share the woman's remembrances of a

345
Arthur Street

"We built this house forty-five years ago, and I've got no plans to leave it."

*7th Annual
Pittsburgh Reunion
in Pittman Park*

time when neighbors painted their houses and cut their yards. They recall no worries of burglaries and violence; Pittsburgh then was "a right grand place" for children.

"Well, we've got to be going," says the young woman at last. "It's a long road to New York. Just wanted to chat with you for awhile."

After the guests leave, the aging woman sits in the center of the room and meditates. Cooling fans whisper against an otherwise clean silence. Finally the woman talks again. She says the old neighbors faithfully elect officeholders who never seem to answer the real needs. Still the old ones endure. They support the woman's quest to bring back the Pittsburgh of another time.

"We need help in turning the neighborhood around," she says, "but sometimes I think this is just a dumping ground for Atlanta. We get people here who were chased out of other places."

She says the police are of little help when trouble comes; if they arrive it always seems too late.

"Anyway, I'm ready for them that try to break in. I've got a dog and gun; I've got the windows barred. Friends say I'd be in a mess if the house caught fire, but I'll take my chances. I'd rather burn up than have somebody come in on me in the night.

"Why don't I move? This is my home and bad people are not going to scare me away.

McDaniel at Mary Street

"Besides, the memories are here; this is my life."

Poncey-Highland

When they came down from Brooklyn five years after they were married, Lisa van den Heuvel and her architect husband, Jim, could not believe their luck. They found a spacious home on a quiet street, a few minutes from downtown. Nestled under great shade trees, the home sat upon a hillock with a large carriage house behind.

"It was wonderful – both the amount of property we could have and the relative costs of the property itself," says Lisa.

It was a friendly place, and Lisa and Jim were to learn they had bought at the right time. Poncey-Highland had been one of those choice middle-class locales that had come upon hard times in the sixties and seventies. Although a few old-timers had stayed put throughout the vicinity's shattery days of transition, neighbors now seemed to be of any age. The van den Heuvels had come upon Poncey at the start of its resurgence. Remarkably, its character – built over the years since 1907 – reappeared essentially intact.

Majestic Restaurant

Right:
Plaza Drugs:
It never closes.

*1009
Ralph McGill
Road*

In the large dining room of the Majestic Restaurant, a relic of Poncey-Highland's art deco days, architect David Grinnell talks above the clatter of dishes and the din of breakfast talk.

"All kinds of people come here," he says. "Not only from Poncey but from all over Atlanta. It's out of times gone by."

A mineral spring rose there that they called "the fountain of youth."

David's friends like his stories of Atlanta and of Poncey-Highland. He can show you the road Sherman marched upon to the Battle of Atlanta, and point out the site of the house in Poncey's Copenhill section where Sherman issued orders. He can tell you that down the street near the old Sears-Roebuck building, workers on a trestle named one of Atlanta's noted thoroughfares for the explorer Ponce de Leon. A mineral spring rose there that they called "the fountain of youth."

*537
Seminole*

David grew up thinking of Atlanta as an important city. He loved going to Atlanta Crackers baseball games at a field near the "fountain," and he went to downtown parades and the state fair in Lakewood Park. Although he enjoyed the amenities of a big city, he knew that Atlanta had rural and suburban advantages that New York, Chicago, and Los Angeles did not have. As a boy, only a few decades ago, he could look three blocks away and see dairy cows grazing.

■ ■ ■

George Mitchell, an Atlanta writer who lives up the street from Lisa and Jim, is without blinders when he talks of his beloved neighborhood. He values the headway homeowners have made at City Hall, but he sees all advances as difficult. How are the neighborhoods to be preserved in the face of the city's growing need for revenue? He is not sure.

*Highland
Elementary School*

*529
Linwood*

"When Maynard Jackson first became mayor, he was a neighborhood man," says Mitchell. "But now, with the pressures to stave off new debt, Jackson is more into the business folks. I think they're not interested in the preservation of neighborhoods. They need tax money; they want wealthy people living downtown."

A block away, on Ponce de Leon Avenue, restaurants and shops give the feeling of a total community. But, like other urbanized parts of the city, the area has drug dealers, street people, and occasionally burglars and robbers.

"Despite gentrification of the area," says Mitchell, author of a popular book about Ponce de Leon Avenue," there are still all types of people in this neighborhood. And although I could do without some of them, such as crack addicts, I really love the diversity.

"This truly is a city that belongs to everyone."

Carter Presidential Center

536 Seminole

Reynoldstown

It seems a sad, forgettable place, but to those who live in its drabness, the settlement is to be cherished – even after 130 years of no outward importance.

Freed slaves found comfort here. Beside the railroad they built crude shotgun houses and tended vegetable gardens. They became rail laborers, carpenters, mechanics, maids, and teachers. They forged a marginal existence and reared children in a cauldron of poverty. Yet the settlement was theirs and, though meager, it was better than bondage. Today, their progeny hold Reynoldstown dear – a trophy to ancient struggles.

In the Lang-Carson Center near the railroad tracks, Young Thomas Hughley, Sr. talks. He is soon to be seventy and has worked since he was nine. He boasts that he never once accepted welfare or took workman's compensation. Only recently did he deign to draw social security. He took no charity even in the desperate days of working at several jobs to feed and educate eleven children.

Hughley led talks when the railroad wanted to put in a "piggyback"

*Flat Shoals
and Stovall*

system next door. The move would have dismantled Reynoldstown's small community center and created new noise. Compromising, the railroad donated a larger building, put up a thirty-five-foot sound barrier, and paid fifty cents a container car to the improvement leagues of both Reynoldstown and bordering Cabbagetown.

*"But the
railroad is the
powerfullest
thing...better
to get what
you can than
to fight them."*

"They were coming anyway," says Hughley. "Some people wanted to fight them; didn't want to cut a deal. But the railroad is the powerfullest thing...better to get what you can than to fight them."

In 1965 Hughley came from a model project, Carver Homes, to live on Manigault Street. Reynoldstown was a healthful place to live then, and Hughley found it cheaper, and more fun for his children.

"The homes back at Carver looked like some fancy place on Peachtree. You had to keep everything spotless. If your children played on the grass, you paid five dollars. If they swung on a door, you paid five dollars. Well, I didn't want them on the playground and out of sight, so I

*Lang-Carson Center,
the heart and soul of the
neighborhood.*

paid a right smart of money keeping them near the house. When you'd call them, sometimes they run across the grass. Five dollars. And I had one boy who liked to swing on the screen doors. Five dollars every time they caught him. That boy was breaking me up.

"I worked at two jobs to pay my first boy's college. Carver Homes charged rent on how much money you made; they didn't allow for the cost to keep you going. So the rent and the fines together ran me out; caused me to move. Been here ever since, and put four children through college. One got a scholarship."

Hughley's oldest son, Young, has a passion for Reynoldstown. For six years he worked as a Broadway theatrical manager; on the side he negotiated talent contracts. One client played in the *Amen* situation comedy. Today he defies all odds: besides heading the Reynoldstown Revitalization Program, he operates an art gallery in the heart of the neighborhood. A curator explains how the gallery survives in the untoward place:

"Young comes from the first family here. Everybody loves the Hughleys and the Hughleys love Reynoldstown. So Young wanted to do his own thing, to make things happen from the place he grew up in – to make the neighborhood come alive from within.

"He wanted to bring art to his own kind. Just today we had kids come in from the church; when time came to go they didn't want to leave.

812 Wylie Street, built by I.P Reynolds, Sr., for whom Reynoldstown is named

Hughley
Art Gallery

Below:
Young T. Hughley, Jr.

"Everybody loves the Hughleys and the Hughleys love Reynoldstown."

And Young's receptions are not snob affairs; to him, art belongs to the people, not just to interior decorators and the northside rich. But investors all around buy black art, and so do corporations like Citicorp and Coca-Cola."

The senior Hughley laughs. He is happy that new ones will carry on after him. Most days he busies himself helping feed seniors and building wood frames for the old ladies who come to make quilts.

"These are my last months. I've fretted about this neighborhood for twenty years, but I'm going home in January." He pantomimes a broad wink: "Just gonna loaf around and beat my wife. We've been together for forty-seven years. Time for somebody else to worry."

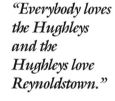

978
Mauldin

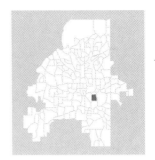

Summerhill

Coca-Cola employees doing volunteer work at the Georgia-Hills Neighborhood Center.

Before an interstate highway disjoined this sixty-block community in the mid-fifties, it was home to twenty thousand residents, mostly Negroes and Jews. There were churches, synagogues, schools, shops, and stores. But after I-20 came and a massive exodus began, there were those who said the old neighborhood – settled by freed slaves and immigrants in the last century – had already begun to decay. They said the well-heeled residents left Summerhill because they had lost voice in its destiny.

When the Atlanta Braves' stadium was built, homeowners again complained. They insisted they had not had a chance to speak, and they looked on helplessly as workers tore down neighboring dwellings. Later, stadium events and parking activity pierced the tranquility of their homes.

By the early nineties Summerhill had shrunk to thirty-five hundred residents, nearly all of them poor and black. Yet, the sparse neighborhood had long since become active when plans for the 1996 Olympics were launched. If the Olympics were to be in their back yard, they would demand to share its dividends.

*Above:
Doug Dean,
director of SNI.*

*Right: Headquarters of Summerhill
Neighborhood, Inc.*

A decade earlier, as proud old Summerhill deteriorated into a slum, Atlanta's leaders tried to save it. After all, the neighborhood had been home to some illustrious people: the families of Sam Massell, former mayor, and Herman Russell, head of the country's fourth largest minority-owned construction company. Also living here were S.W. Walker, founder of Pilgrim Life Insurance Company, and Leon Eplan, head of city planning.

Even $173 million for urban renewal did not help; the neighborhood plummeted and housing projects became riddled with murderers, rapists, drug pushers, and dope addicts. Solid citizens shook their

738 Cherokee

heads; they told each other that money would not be enough. Said one, "The only people who live here now are those that can't afford to move somewhere else." The soul of Summerhill seemed to be dying.

Yet there were those like Hattie Harrison who contested Summerhill's fate. It was a place she had loved for seventy years; if it sank, she would go down with it. Shouldering a baseball bat, she patrolled the housing project and openly defied criminals who taunted and threatened her. Dwellers there saw the slight, grandmotherly battler as a kind of Joan of Arc. They quietly celebrated with her when at last the Atlanta Housing Authority agreed to let tenants own the project. Big money had failed, but earnest, angry, organized little people might drive out lowlife and reclaim the complex.

Shouldering a baseball bat, she patrolled the housing project and openly defied criminals who taunted and threatened her.

Another hero is Douglas Dean – former legislator, optimist, and indefatigable head of the non-profit group that would rebuild rundown houses, set up minority businesses, and bring Summerhill back to the vibrant scene of his boyhood.

A small, quiet person, he may leave his office on a Saturday and join a volunteer group to clean buildings and grounds. Shirt hanging out and baseball cap too large on his head, Dean appears unheroic. But he talks softly and easily at the center of earnest, informal groups. He counsels neighbors, finds jobs for out-of-work people, seeks to ease their problems, and badgers friends in high places for help.

He remembers that Summerhill once had four major grocery stores; when he goes to meetings today people ask about getting a store back in the neighborhood. "The truth of the matter," says Dean, "is that a grocery store or drug store is not going to locate here until Summerhill has buying power. Right now it would be unfair to ask [a retail business] to come in here when seventy percent of the people are on social security or some government subsidy."

Even on the weekends the phone keeps ringing in Dean's modest office. Street plans and architects' drawings cover the walls and spill onto the floor. He says his group is leveraging its plan by sharing it with people all over the country, that the Urban Land Institute has come in and said the

137
Glenwood Street

Martin Street
Church of God

Summerhill blueprint is a solid plan. He believes the plan can be a model for other inner-city neighborhoods throughout the country.

Dean thinks Summerhill will flourish in the nineties: "We've got to have a partnership with the corporate community, the education community. This is not a place to raise a family now. We don't have the schools; we don't have the churches like when I was growing up here."

He says the crux of the planning is to "re-neighbor" the community, to return it to a place of mixed races and income groups, a district with power to buy and attract commercial interests.

"The majority of those who have stayed here want to die here," he said. "I hope they live to see what the neighborhood is going to become: people with economic and political influence, a place that will have churches, schools, playgrounds, businesses."

He says the answer to the problem in Summerhill is simple: "Bring the people back."

"The majority of those who have stayed here want to die here."

Martin Street Plaza Housing Project

738 Hill Street

Sweet Auburn

On a sunbathed Sunday morning in July, crisply dressed churchgoers cross the hexagonal pavers along Auburn Avenue's sidewalks. They nod to one another and speak in soft voices. They are reverential and solemn – proud women herding clusters of grandchildren, young married couples exuding freshness and hope, old people poking canes upon the pavers. Most climb the flight of granite steps that lead to Big Bethel's sanctuary. Some disappear into the lower level.

"A few get here late and go to the basement," says a sprightly matriarch. "They come up from the inside so people will think they're not late, like they've been to the downstairs services."

Big Bethel African Methodist Episcopal Church

94

*"At night
it's mostly
street people
and them that's
up to no good
that walk these
sidewalks."*

Outside, a church guard stands on the corner of Auburn and Butler. He is in his fifties and he came home to Atlanta from Chicago years ago. He says he does not think the public should blame the president for the current economic slump.

"One man's not responsible for this mess," he says. "We're all guilty. I'm not necessarily for the president...never voted but once and that was for McCarthy. Haven't felt like voting because politicians are all alike and I don't want to help any of them get elected."

A small, trim, and handsome elderly woman comes out of the church. She says she does not have time to talk much, that she must call her sick husband from a phone booth across the street.

"A woman's first duty is to her man," she says, "But I want to speak to you. When I see curious people outside Big Bethel I come up to welcome them."

Royal Peacock Club

The guard and the churchgoer talk of Sweet Auburn, a district that got its name nearly sixty years ago from John Wesley Dobbs, grandfather of Atlanta's mayor, Maynard Jackson.

"Sweet Auburn's not what it used to be," says the guard. "It's a shadow of its old self, and at night it's mostly street people and them that's up to no good that walk these sidewalks."

He points up the street where tall buildings of glass and granite glitter in the sunlight.

"Look at all that steel going up on the edge of town. That'll be a library. New buildings soon will be built down this street. One day this part of Sweet Auburn will be gone."

"We let it happen," says the old woman. "Just like you smoking that cigarette there. You know it's not good for you, but you still smoke. If

you'd saved all the money you've spent on cigarettes, you'd not have to work part-time. Problem with all of us – this country and all – is that we don't produce and save. Other countries are going to eat us up, and we do nothing about it but maybe smoke cigarettes."

The guard shakes his head and smiles; he looks down at his newly lighted cigarette and then drops it, crushing it beneath his foot.

Soon the woman must leave, but the talk of Sweet Auburn lingers. She and her amiable new adversary know that the district flourished in its younger days when *Fortune* once called it "the richest Negro street in the world."

He began to employ Mahatma Gandhi's "soul-force" to edge black brothers and sisters onto a new plateau of freedom and vision.

On Auburn Avenue an ex-slave crafted an enterprise that was to become the second largest black-run insurance company in the nation. Near it was formed in 1928 the *Daily World*, said to be the first daily newspaper for blacks in the country. In the next year, a few blocks to the east and up the hill, a black child was born who was to absorb the rhetoric of his religious father. As he grew up he began to employ Mahatma Gandhi's "soul-force" to edge blacks onto a new plateau of freedom and vision. Martin Luther King, Jr. and the elder King preached in Sweet Auburn's Ebenezer Baptist Church, which with Big Bethel and Wheat Street Baptist molded the ethical thinking of Atlanta's African-American world.

There is a bleakness and sadness that pervades Sweet Auburn, but it

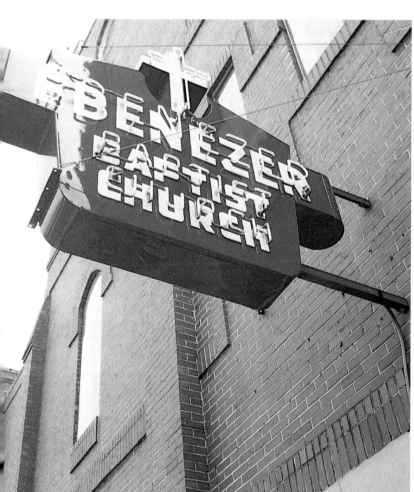

Church of Martin Luther King, Sr. and Jr.

Right:
Tomb of Martin Luther King, Jr.

was the center of hope for black people. They could not buy a dinner along Peachtree, but four restaurants in Sweet Auburn made Saturday nights deliciously memorable. One of these places, the Royal Peacock, a night spot in the tradition of Harlem's Cotton Club, brought noted names from the world of black entertainment – B.B. King, Ray Charles, and Aretha Franklin among them. From the corner of Big Bethel, one can look a block west to see an old marquee and know that the night before there played inside the Royal Peacock's dim chambers the throbbing, honeyed sounds of rhythm and blues.

Tuxedo Park

A tour coach creeps along the winding roads of Tuxedo Park and stops before the incomparable Swan House. Chatty passengers bring out cameras. The coach moves on to other avenues and past homes of the people who drive the city's commerce – among them, the Richardsons, the Kennedys, the Fuquas, the Rollinses. At the gate of Bobby Jones's languishing estate, passengers stretch to see the manor beyond the putting green. The older ones recall when Jones was to golfing what Babe Ruth was to baseball and Charles Lindbergh to flying. At the Ivan Allen compound, the sightseers peer through tall pines and oaks to view the placid loveliness of homes and grounds. Some of the tourists are well traveled; they have seen the storied mansions of Europe and homes of the rich and famous of Beverly Hills, Grosse Point, and Great Neck. But they know that upon these rolling red acres of Georgia is a domain rarely equaled for sheer beauty.

541 Paces Ferry Road. Home designed by Philip Shutze.

3425 Tuxedo Road, home of all-time golfing great, the late Robert Tyre (Bobby) Jones, Jr.

Right: Bobby Jones

Mary Norwood – who lives on Habersham Road and manages a business while fighting for her views – is among those who who want strict zoning for Tuxedo Park. She knows that as older families pass from the scene, their large estates are often sold to developers who see profit in the excess land. A new road may be carved through a fifteen-acre parcel, leaving the manor intact, but dividing the other land into many lots.

Mary admits there are other sides to the issue. Opposing views, for instance, come from developers; they sell to executives who aspire to the area but do not want the expense of a large estate. There are those people – including owners within Tuxedo Park – who would deplore new zoning. They say no rules should direct what they do with their property.

"Add to this," says Mary, "that City Hall wants new revenues; they get more taxes from nine homes on a piece of land than from one home on the same land.

Cherokee Town Club. Original acreage bought by parents of Louise Richardson Allen in the early 1920s.

Calhoun-Thornwell House. 1922-23 Pinestream Road.

"But many neighbors know that once this area is carved up, its charm will be gone. Tour buses probably won't be coming through anymore. But despite damage already done, this garden is still one of the wonders of the world."

In the sunken living room where she overlooks her gardens and a greensward that sweeps on to Nancy Creek, Louise Allen talks of art, of nature, of Atlanta.

She says that people have to work together to make a first-class city; that Atlanta is a strong art community; that even Georgia Tech, an engineering school, has a new theater.

4047 Tuxedo Road

100

*3795
Tuxedo Road*

**Tuxedo Park
makes up
much of the
Allens' lives,
but so does
the whole of
the city.**

To her, nature is a therapy. She stayed outdoors the day before and says that is why she slept well. In a few hours she and husband Ivan will leave for the stadium. As long-time mayor, Ivan helped bring both the football Falcons and the baseball Braves to Atlanta. Tuxedo Park makes up much of the Allens' lives, but so does the whole of the city.

Louise's family moved out from West Peachtree when she was a young girl. Nearby, the Swan House was built for her mother's brother, Edward Inman, who died less than five years later. Louise's father was among Atlantans who early in the century built summer homes in the area of Paces Ferry and Northside Drive.

Downtown was growing northward, and the noise of steam shovels was incessant along West Peachtree where Louise lived with her parents.

*Governor's Mansion.
391 West Paces
Ferry Road.*

When the Biltmore Hotel was going up, the family finally decided to move to Tuxedo Park. They built a home Louise's mother called Broadlands, and they watched the neighborhood grow grandly.

In the early days, the Paces Ferry area developed slowly. There were few amenities of the city, but the land was a botanical Eden. Louise remembers that when the father sold his first lot in Tuxedo Park he opened a bottle of champagne. He had come from Vicksburg as a young man to the Cotton States Exposition; like many others, he found

3668 Tuxedo Road. George Woodruff house.

3640 Tuxedo Road. "Windcrofte," the Robert Woodruff house.

*3703
Tuxedo Road*

his future in the climate and the land. He never went back to Vicksburg.

Louise and Ivan grew up with a generation of Tuxedo Park people who helped steer Atlanta's cultural growth. Soon after Ivan became mayor, a jetliner crashed at Orly, France, killing 106 Atlantans on an art tour. It was the worst single commercial air tragedy the world had yet known.

That Sunday afternoon, cars lined the streets of Tuxedo Park. The mayor flew to Paris knowing that he would count neighbors among the dead, many of them lifetime friends. He wondered, too, if Atlanta's strong cultural ambitions would survive.

In their shock, friends told one another that the city's art movement perished at Orly. Even before the crash, a bond issue for a new museum had been beaten. Now prospects were even bleaker; but Atlantans set up a fund which led to the erection of the Atlanta Memorial Arts Center. The people of France sent a bronze casting by Rodin. The figure stands inside the building, its head bowed in perpetuity.

Vine City

Except for time in World War II when he flew with the Tuskegee Airmen, George Prather has spent his life in the brick bungalow his parents built in the twenties.

Pausing often to stroke his demanding, twenty-two-year-old black cat, he reminisces:

"It was a great neighborhood, a middle-class place. We went to school, to church. We were law-abiding. If you carried anything other than a Boy Scout knife, the rest of us would have nothing to do with you. The exclusion was pretty effective.

"At a party guys might 'spike the punch,' but cocaine, marijuana, acid – never heard of that stuff.

"Vine City was a good-looking neighborhood when I was coming along. Postal workers, railroad firemen, educators, porters, chauffeurs – they were at the top of the economic ladder. Had nice homes, educated their children. School was the number-one priority. You had to go to school."

234 Sunset Street, home of Martin Luther King, Jr. and wife, Coretta, when he was killed in Memphis.

As a youth, Prather attended the "lab school," and was taught by Atlanta University student teachers. In high school, he knew a boy "about three grades down" whom everybody called M.L.

"M.L. was a normal, red-blooded American boy who had a BB gun and a slingshot along with the rest of us. Played football, softball...in the Boy Scouts.

"Years later I was down in Montgomery, and a lady there learned I was from Atlanta. She seemed disappointed that I didn't know Martin Luther King. I studied for a minute and then it hit me. She was talking about M.L. His name at birth, you know, was Michael."

Around the corner on the next block, Martin Luther and Coretta King bought a house and added to it. It was their home when King was slain in Memphis.

On that same avenue, Sunset, are some of Vine City's largest and best-preserved homes. But up a hillock and just off Sunset is the showplace of Vine City – the home of Alonzo Herndon, a man born in slavery, later to found the second largest black-owned insurance firm in the country.

After Atlanta's great fire of 1917, many burned-out families in Sweet Auburn moved to Vine City where college campuses lay just inside its boundary and spread over the West End area. The institutions heavily influenced neighbors – economically, politically, morally.

"The normal way to live was to go to church," Prather recalls. "You had to go to church and go to school. If you didn't, brother, you are in deep trouble at home." He willingly embraced the ethic. He attended Clark College, played football, and later ran a business that served the academic community.

Vine City – anchored by the Herndon mansion and settled snug beside the largest concentration of black colleges in the world – became both a ghetto and a haven. Isolated from real opportunity in Reconstruction years, neighbors hewed out an existence from jobs and enterprises shunned by whites. They did not dream for themselves but for their children. Churches, schools, and workplaces formed their unity.

Above: Grocery at Sunset and Simpson

Right: 101 Sunset

"Seems like every street had its own community club," says Prather. "But the clubs existed just for people to meet now and then. Couldn't do much else. Too busy making a living. When they got home they had to cook and feed the children...make the children do their homework. But World War II changed a lot of things. Some good, some bad."

Churches, clubs, and other institutions still operate, but the old ethic is tarnished. Wildcat fences gird multifamily apartments. Iron bars are clapped upon houses and even campus buildings. Coarse and brutal ways affront the upward culture of George Prather's younger days. Although generations have died and their children gone away, there remains a small core of enlightened successors, young and old, who seem unconquerable.

Prather belongs to a black church group that has formed a development corporation. Members appealed to the Georgia-Pacific Corporation to finance two hundred houses. "We laid to rest the myth that nobody would buy a house here," he says. "Fifty new homes have been sold, and Georgia-Pacific calls it 'Project Hope,' and that's just what it is."

"We used to believe in one another," says Prather. "Went to church, went to school, obeyed our parents.

"America needs to get back to that."

*Morris Brown
College*

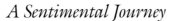

A Sentimental Journey

Virginia-Highland

It is a setting for Fitzgerald and Wolfe. Trendy frequenters of its boutiques, lounges, and outdoor cafes evoke images of expatriates on the Champs-Elysees. Ghosts of flappers, sheiks, and ramblin' wrecks pass beneath the canopies.

The picture seen today is much like those taken with old folding cameras. Visitors are delighted that the place still exudes the magic of Lindbergh, Pickford, Valentino, Bobby Jones.

A young woman returning from New York City looked here for a dwelling she could afford – one that would remind her of the Roaring-Twenties home where she grew up.

"The classics were all around," she says. "It was just a matter of finding a house with my name on it. Then they showed me an enchanting place with archways – one to the dining room, one to the kitchen. I knew standing there: I must have it, possess it, own it."

Time scarcely alters facades of either the stores on Virginia and Highland

Artists at Summer Festival

Right:
Sidewlk cafe on North Highland Avenue

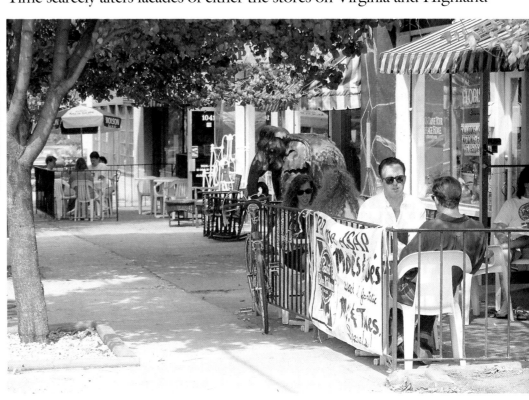

108

*North Highland
and Virginia avenues
circa 1920*

*They enjoy
the life of
villagers
from another
time.*

avenues or the homes of this, the largest intown residential area.

"Most people like what they've bought," says a ten-year resident. "They don't want to change the way their own house looks because it might impact the whole area. Neighbors are mindful of keeping the place the way it was. When we need to expand, we fill in basement space or add rooms out back. The fronts look pretty much as they always did."

Those who work may be no farther than twenty minutes from their offices. The quick commute gives them more time to shop nearby, work in yards, stroll in the parks, go to meetings. Sometimes neighbors rope off a street for a block party; they bring lawn chairs and sit with newcomers. They enjoy the life of villagers from another time.

*1055 Greencove
Avenue*

The Adair Mansion on Rupley Avenue

Because residents get together often, it is no surprise that they talk of civic problems. Once more than two hundred residents turned out to discuss a parking issue. Nyna Gentry remembers the gathering as "volatile," a time when homeowners and restaurant and bar operators talked tensely with one another.

"We're glad to have visitors," says Nyna. "They come from all around – people from Cobb and Gwinnett counties, bright students from Atlanta University and Emory. But a few ignore no-parking signs, jam the streets, park on lawns, block driveways, or maybe damage shrubbery. They sometimes sound horns, break bottles, or shout late at night.

"For those who live close by, this can be a burden. But bar owners and restaurateurs say many owners bought here knowing they are near the activity. The disagreement goes on. We'll have rough times, but finally we'll find some way to resolve the issue."

Children in Atkins Park

1153
St. Charles Place

Nyna speaks with assurance, knowing how friends once helped stop highway I-485 from cleaving the neighborhood. Like most residents she enjoys the commercial district and its visitors.

"You've got hardware stores close by and supermarkets just outside. You've got a convenience store that's nice when you need little things. Clerks carry groceries to cars of the elderly, even take food to their homes when they're sick."

In the 1890s a few houses were built along the tracks of the Nine-Mile Circle trolley, where access walkways are still visible. The catalyst for the village building boom, however, was a new bridge to Piedmont Park, built before World War I. The area filled in with period homes, and little since has been done to spoil the classic American character of the neighborhood.

840
Virginia Circle

West End

It is a warm autumn day, and young men on stage rap thunderously. A Harlem Globetrotter challenges boys and girls to compete in a free-throw game for charity. Throughout spacious Howell Park, visitors stand in groups or sit on blankets and folding chairs. They roast wieners or chicken over charcoal; they offer newspapers and hand out pamphlets. It is the annual West End Festival, "...a celebration of history, a call for unity and cultural commitment."

In an open tent, forty-year-old Janice White Sikes – librarian, history buff, civic leader, and mother – rests from volunteer chores. From a hundred yards distant, the rap music at times smothers her speech. She shakes her head slowly and smiles.

679
Peeples Street

"Youth. Let's face it. In America there's fear of the young who have nowhere to go, nothing to do. Nobody wants kids just roaming the street."

A handsome boy steals up and cups his hands over Janice's eyes. She turns to see her teenage son.

"Your haircut," she gasps.

*"Some people
spend a lot
of time saying
what they
can't do."*

The son is apprehensive; fleetingly he searches for any sign that will tell him the mother approves. Someone says that at least the barber didn't cut slogans into the hair. Wearily Janice waves him away, saying that maybe she will get used to it. The boy beams. He blows a kiss as he dashes off.

A man and woman wave from a passing car. Janice says they are one reason she and her husband Dann, a television producer, came to West End.

"She's from Sweden; he's from New York. Both are artists. They came here long ago wanting to help create a cultural community of intellectuals and working people. Some people spend a lot of time saying what they can't do; now there are two who just do it."

Soon talk turns to West End's history:

"Joel Chandler Harris, author of the Uncle Remus stories, lived here. He considered himself a working person. Everyday he would take the trolley downtown and go to work for the *Constitution*. In the 1906 riot, he opened his home to friends of color. The Wren's Nest was a safe harbor; that's rarely known history. Also, few know that in 1876 West End was half black, half white. Jim Crow laws changed that, and after the First World War, blacks began moving out."

Janice says she has always studied history, that her grandparents owned property in the mid-nineteenth century, that being a librarian is an outgrowth of the way she grew up.

"I'm surrounded by people who read. They give me books for Christmas; I give them books. People here have always tended to be writers and craftsmen. Three of our neighbors are carpenters, and that's no different from the old days. There were bricklayers, educators, blacksmiths, seamstresses, draymen – skilled, working-class people. Old values are still here, have never left. Some get upset about West End's history; they pretend the neighborhood was once rich. But people here went to work; they still go to work."

Friends drop by – a chic and amiable woman who does interior designs and heads West End's cleanup programs; a man who once ran down a

*Home of
Joel Chadler Harris,
creator of
Uncle Remus.*

robber; a pair of teenage girls. Excitedly they talk of a poetry-reading, of African-American art in the old Hammond House, of books and music. Janice says she is a West End chauvinist. ("There are lots of people like me.") She does not care, she says, whether a person is on welfare or living in a big house. "They're excited about living in West End. It's a sense of pride."

"Old values are still here, have never left."

She says West End is a mix of everything – incomes, races, interests. She talks of Wade Burns, a Virginian who brought his architectural skills to West End, bought old houses, renovated them, and placed wrought-iron fences around them as a mark of his work.

"I always kid Wade," says Janice. "I tell him he's my kind. Like me, he was raised in a family of business people; they owned a brick company and made things happen. He started a kind of movement here.

"What you've got to understand about West End is that its leadership

698
Peeples Street

has nothing to do with color: It's about vision; it's about love; it's about people saying things to each other in their heart, whether you agree with them or not. There is a tolerance for that. For a long time we had a way of saying, 'West End Works.'

"And it's still that way."

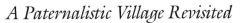
Whittier Mills

Relic of the demolished mill complex

Three years after the poet John Greenleaf Whittier died in 1892, a distant relative came to Georgia from New England to set up a textile plant beside the Chattahoochee River.

W.R.B. "Boss" Whittier chose a site for his factory and village on a gentle roll of land between the Southern Railroad and the river. Thus he took advantage of transportation and abundant water; but even more critical to his family's profits was cheap labor that included women and children. These poverty-blanched Georgians would toil twelve hours a day under foremen brought from the family's enterprise centered in Lowell, Massachusetts.

In that time there were few protective laws for workers in the South, but Whittier's son, Sid, born the day the mill opened, later wrote that there were a hundred people waiting for every job available.

Boss Whittier acquired thirty acres of valley land from the nearby Chattahoochee Brick Company. With "the finest hard brick" he

In the village many lived better than when, as sharecroppers, they plowed the poor, eroded earth of rural North Georgia.

constructed a 40,000-square-foot mill. On a nearby crescent hill he built scores of wood-frame cottages for his new workers.

For his own, Whittier erected an imposing home at the highest point in the village. Here he could look down to the factory from which he piped steam to warm his family. On a wooded bluff he built rambling frame quarters for family members and other executives. These places survive today, but Boss Whittier's mansion, called Hedgerows, burned to the ground in the late 1970s.

Elizabeth Ann Gignilliat, in front of her home at 3 Spring Circle. Her mother, Laura Lieberman, is a neighborhood advocate and enthusiast.

At the turn of the century, Whittier's workers produced window-sash cords and fire-hose casings. They earned one silver dollar a day, a wage that even a hundred years ago seemed unfair. Nevertheless, families of the time zealously protected their jobs and handed them down to daughters and sons. In the village many lived better than when, as share-croppers, they plowed the poor, eroded earth of rural North Georgia.

Workers paid a dollar and a half a week for rent and utilities, and the mill painted and repaired their houses and maintained their yards without cost. Employees charged dry goods, groceries, and hardware at the company store; they left their little ones to be cared for at the settlement house. In their meager off-times they attended church nearby, and by the bandstand spread quilts upon the grass to listen to neighbors play fiddles and guitars. In later years they cheered as their baseball teams competed against those of other North Georgia cotton mills.

By 1971 foreign competitors had killed the Whittier enterprise, and the factory shut down. In 1988 new owners razed the main mill building, but they left standing a three-story brick tower, the tumbled-down remains of the company store, and the carpenter shop.

After the mill closed, retired employees bought both original houses and those built in 1926. A new vitality came into the settlement when young buyers found the village to be a good place to live. Together the old and new formed a neighborhood association. Its central goal was to gain historical recognition for the quiet and picturesque old village.

Resurgens

No metropolis in America survives without scars of its expansion. In their crucibles, some cities surrender too easily to the forces of growth. Yet, Atlanta – perhaps because of its rise from a scorched earth, or because it was always driven by a youthful spirit – seems to absorb growth with intrinsic poise.

When a community is born, its people huddle around the central core. As the town spreads, wealthy citizens move outward and call their new suburbs "parks," "terraces," "gardens," and "hills." While they cherish the city, they wish to separate their private lives from the ferment of commerce. Yet, laborers and the poor seem always to live in the shadows of a city until progress evicts them.

Since mid-century, many wealthy homeowners have learned to insulate themselves from Atlanta's outward march and from the expansion of new neighborhoods. They simply move beyond the city's boundaries and choke off its spread by forming new towns. In this way, they avoid attending the ills of a sprawling metropolis. A city's needs are left to its commerce, its small taxpayers, and to the affluent ones who can remain in the city because their large estates are beyond encroachment. Indeed, in these pockets, estate holders do provide welcome money; but, because there are so few, they can provide only a fraction of the city's enormous monetary needs.

So drastic were Atlanta's neighborhood changes in the fifties and sixties that many large homes became tenements, and smaller homes were rented or sold at low prices. Proud old neighborhoods tottered and tax revenues fell drastically. Only the influx of new industries and institutions could bolster a city largely abandoned by the people who had tended its gardens and contributed to its coffers.

Happily, a new Atlanta renaissance germinated in the seventies. Neglected venues revived under the stimulus of creative adventurers. A new pride emerged in both wealthy and modest neighborhoods. Long-buried tendrils poked through and spring seemed to return.

The revival seems to have saved the neighborhoods, but its energy and force tempered the growth of the city. A new consciousness lives, and homeowners are active; they battle new taxes; they block superhighways; they confront developers who want to cut into large properties and erect multifamily buildings. Ironically, in the course of saving Atlanta's neighborhoods, these activated residents throw up obstacles to the advancement of the city's commerce.

In much of America, neighborhoods give way to expanding municipal needs; but Atlantans see their city as unique – a blend of home and work, of neighborhood and city. They want the city to grow and prosper so long as the enhancements do not threaten the integrity of their neighborhoods.

People who live in fine homes and cultivate lush gardens understandably have pride in their surroundings; but, surprisingly, those who live amid poverty and danger also love and defend their neighborhoods. Because of such attachment in all neighborhoods, the crown of an ever-resurging Atlanta again rests uneasily upon its head.

Bibliography

References – Books

Atlanta Urban Design Commission. *Atlanta: Triumph of a People.* Atlanta, 1987.

Cooper, Walter G. *The Cotton States & International Exposition & South,* c. 1896.

Evans, Ivor H. *Brewer's Dictionary of Phrase & Fable.* New York: Harper & Row, 1981.

Jackson, Kenneth T. *Crabgrass Frontier.* New York, Oxford: Oxford University Press, 1985.

Mitchell, William R. & Martin, Van Jones. *Classic Atlanta.* New Orleans: Martin St. Martin Publishing Company.

Pyron, Darden Asbury. *Southern Daughter.* New York, Oxford: Oxford University Press, 1991.

Shavin, Norman & Galphin, Bruce. *Atlanta: Triumph of a People.* Atlanta: Capricorn Corporation, 1982.

Spalding, Phinizy. *Georgia: The WPA Guide to Its Towns and Countryside.* Columbia: University of South Carolina, 1990.

References – Newspapers, Periodicals, Studies.

Ansley Park Civic Association. *Historic Living in Ansley Park,* 1982.

Atlanta Journal/Constitution. *"Orly Crash".* June 3, 1962.

Atlanta Journal/Constitution. *"Mozley Park".* February 1, 1992.

Atlanta Journal/Constitution. *"Summerhill".* June 10, 1992.

Inman Park Festival & Tour of Homes Brochure, 1992.

Jones, Tommy H. *Inman Park History and Architecture,* 1992.

Manly, Howard. *"Bittersweet Auburn".* Atlanta Magazine.

Morningside/Lenox Park Newsletter. Vol. II, No. 3, 1990.

Mueller, Richard P. *Chronology of Adair Park,* 1991.

National Registry of Historic Places (Nomination Forms for Ansley Park, Brookwood Hills, Candler Park, Garden Hills, Grant Park, Inman Park, Tuxedo Park, Virginia-Highland).

Peachtree Hills Matters. Vol. 4, No. 4, July 1991.

Rooney, Don & Leiberman, Laura. *History of Whittier Mills Village,* 1992.

Index